Crossroads Café

ASSESSMENT A

The publication of *Crossroads Café* was directed by the members of the Heinle & Heinle Secondary and Adult ESL Publishing Team.

Editorial Director:	Roseanne Mendoza
Production Services Coordinator:	Mike Burggren
Market Development Director:	Jonathan Boggs

Also participating in the publication of the program were:

Vice President and Publisher, ESL:	Stanley Galek
Developmental Editor:	K. Lynn Savage
Production Editor:	Maryellen Killeen
Manufacturing Coordinator:	Mary Beth Hennebury
Full Service Design and Production:	PC&F, Inc.

Manufactured in the United States of America.

ISBN: 0-8384-8070-5

Heinle & Heinle is a division of International Thomson Publishing, Inc.

Photo Credits
Episodes 1, 2, 3, 4, 5, 6, 9, 10, 13, 14, 16, 17, 18: Stanley Newton
Episodes 7, 8, 11, 12, 15, 19, 20, 21, 22, 23, 24, 25, 26: Jane O'Neal

Crossroads Café
ASSESSMENT A

Elizabeth Minicz

Kathleen Santopietro Weddel

Kathryn Powell

Lydia Omori

Anna Cuomo

HEINLE & HEINLE PUBLISHERS

I T P *An International Thomson Publishing Company*

Boston, Massachusetts 02116 U.S.A.

New York • London • Bonn • Boston • Detroit • Madrid • Melbourne • Mexico City • Paris •
Singapore • Tokyo • Toronto • Washington • Albany, NY • Belmont, CA • Cincinnati, OH

Acknowledgments

Rigorous review by members of the National Academic Council contributed to the initial design as well as the philosophical underpinnings of the products: Fiona Armstrong, Office of Adult and Continuing Education, New York City Board of Education; Janet Buongiorno, Adult Literacy Enhancement Center, Edison, New Jersey; Yvonne Cadiz, Adult and Community Education Program, Hillsborough County Public Schools, Florida; the late Jim Dodd, Bureau of Adult and Community Education, Department of Education, Florida; Chela Gonzalez, Metropolitan Adult Education Program, San Jose, California; Chip Harman, United States Information Agency, Washington, D.C.; Edwina Hoffman, Dade County Public Schools, Florida; Maggie Steinz, Illinois State Board of Education; Dennis Terdy, Adult Learning Resource Center, Des Plaines, Illinois; Inaam Mansour, Arlington Education and Employment Program, Arlington, Virginia; Fortune Valenty, Perth Amboy Public Schools, New Jersey; Kathleen Santopietro Weddel, Colorado Department of Education.

In addition to review by the National Academic Council, the assessment portions of Crossroads Café benefited from review by the following individuals: Frances Butler, Center for the Study of Evaluation, University of California, Los Angeles; Rob Jenkins, Rancho Santiago Community College District, Orange, California; Mary Ann Losee, Horizonte Instrucional and Training Center, Salt Lake City, Utah; Deborah Weir, El Camino College, Torrance, California.

Liz would like to thank a great team—Lynn, Kathryn, Anna, and Lydia—for their grace under pressure. She also thanks Eric, Christa, and Ian for being tolerant of their mom's writing schedule.

Kathleen would like to thank Lynn Savage for asking her to participate as a co-author; her supportive compliments are like a friendship pearl sewn on a beautiful dress.

Kathryn, Lydia, and Anna would all like to thank Liz Minicz for inviting them to participate in the project and for her supportive leadership. Kathryn would like to thank Madeleine and Francis D. Powell, her first and best teachers; Barb Singer for her word-processing feats; Miryam and Sarah for putting up with her divided attention; and Ahmed, for these 10 years at a cultural crossroads.

Lydia would like to first thank God for all good things and people, and especially for George and Rei (dad and mom) and Greg Sahli (husband). Greg has the patience of a saint, and his assistance was most appreciated.

Anna dedicates her efforts to her parents, Salvatore and Annunziata Cuomo, who have taught her good sense and what is important in life.

Contents

Introduction vi

Masters
   Learner Log ix
   Writing Assessment x
   Scoresheet xi

Guidelines for Holistic Scoring
   Speaking
      Photo Stories xii
      ✪ xiii
      ✪✪ xiv
      ✪✪✪ xv
     Language Structure ✪, ✪✪, and ✪✪✪ xvi
     Writing
      ✪ xvii
      ✪✪ xviii
      ✪✪✪ xix
     Critical Thinking (all levels) xx

Unit 1   Opening Day 1–1

Unit 2   Growing Pains 2–1

Unit 3   Worlds Apart 3–1

Unit 4   Who's the Boss? 4–1

Unit 5   Lost and Found 5–1

Unit 6   Time Is Money 6–1

Unit 7   Fish Out of Water 7–1

Unit 8   Family Matters 8–1

Unit 9   Rush to Judgment 9–1

Unit 10   Let the Buyer Beware 10–1

Unit 11   No Vacancy 11–1

Unit 12   Turning Points 12–1

Unit 13   Trading Places 13–1

Introduction

This assessment package provides tools for both informal and formal assessments. For the informal assessment tools, there are no suggestions for scoring. For the formal assessment tools, scoring systems that evaluate the quality of the language are provided.

Some tools work with all proficiency levels while others are level specific.

Tools designed for all proficiency levels
- Learner Log
- Learner Checklist
- Instructor Checklist

Tools designed for specific levels (Photo Stories, SPL 3[1], Beginning Low[2]; Worktext ✪, SPL 4, Beginning High; Worktext ✪✪, SPL 5, Intermediate Low; Worktext ✪✪✪, SPL 6, Intermediate High)
- Listening
- Speaking
- Language Structure
- Critical Thinking
- Reading
- Writing

A description of each tool follows.

Learner Log. This is an informal, unscored tool that encourages learner reflection. The questions focus on language acquired.

Learner Checklist. This is an informal, unscored, tool that lists the four competencies under "In this unit you will . . ." on each unit opener page: 1) a language function; 2) a life skills reading; 3) a writing task; 4) cultural knowledge. Learners indicate how easy or difficult they feel each competency is for them.

Instructor Checklist. These are the same four competencies as on the Learner Checklist. However, in this case, the instructor rates the quality of the learner's language for each competency.

Used together, the two checklists can guide a discussion between the learner and the instructor to determine the future learning focus.

---

[1]SPL, Student Performance Level, as defined by the Mainstream English Language Training Project (Office of Refugee Resettlement).

[2]Beginning Low, Beginning High, Intermediate Low, Intermediate High as defined by the English-as-a-Second-Language Model Standards for Adult Education Programs (Sacramento, CA: California Department of Education Bureau of Publications)

Listening. These require audio- (Photo Stories) or video- (Worktexts) tapes and worksheets for learners to record answers. They are graded by points, one point for each correct answer. The answer keys are available in the Notes to the Teacher sections of each unit. Scripts follow the Notes to the Teacher in each unit.

Tasks vary by level, as follows.

Photo Stories (audiotape): Learners hear a sentence and indicate which of two pictures matches the sentence.

Worktexts (videotape): Passages are the same for each proficiency level; they usually have two or more speakers, and run less than one minute for each passage. The questions asked and the amount of detail needed to answer vary by level.

- ✪: Questions focus on the main topic or message of the passage. For example, What are they talking about? How does X feel? Learners find answers not only from the words spoken, but also from what they see.
- ✪✪: Questions focus on finding specific information in the passage that supports the main topic. Learners need to understand the language used in the passage to answer the questions.
- ✪✪✪: Questions focus on inference and drawing conclusions. Learners must interpret meaning, not just understand the words they hear.

Speaking. General directions are on the Student Worksheets. Additional details are in the Notes to the Teacher sections. These are scored holistically. Instructors may score *live* responses or have students record their answers on audiotapes, which are then scored outside of instructional time. Scoring guidelines are provided on pages xii–xiv. Tasks vary by level.

- Photo Stories: Learners respond to a general question that is related to the title/topic of a specific episode. Learners' answers are derived by watching, not just listening, to the video and *reading* the pictures in the Photo Story, not just the words.
- ✪: Learners talk about a frame from the Photo Story that is reproduced on the worksheet. Input is predominantly visual and output is in words and phrases.
- ✪✪: Learners talk about episode themes and how they relate to their lives. Probes are printed on worksheets, but may also be aural if the instructor is scoring *live* responses. Output is in sentences.
- ✪✪✪: Learners explain the titles or tell the stories. Probes are printed on worksheets, but may also be aural if the instructor is scoring *live* responses. Output is at the multiple-sentence level; that is, the learner produces a string of related sentences.

Language Structure. These tools are for learners using the Worktext, since the Photo Stories do not provide practice with functions or grammatical structures. The section is scored holistically. Scoring guidelines are provided on page xv. For each level, learners respond in writing to questions on the respective worksheets. Tasks vary by level.

- ✪: Questions are for only the first structure presented in Your New Language. Output, at the word and phrase level, demonstrates understanding of the function/question.
- ✪✪: Questions are for structures presented in the two-star activity in Your New Language as well as the structure presented in the one-star. Responses should be complete sentences, demonstrating control of the structure.
- ✪✪✪: Learners often write questions as well as responses to questions.

Reading. There are two types of tasks, one for the Photo Stories and one for the Worktext.

- Photo Stories: Learners complete a sentence of text that describes a photo by choosing one of three options. They are scored by points, one point for each correct answer. The answer keys are available in the unit-specific Notes to the Teacher sections.
- Worktext: This tool mirrors the task in the In Your Community section of the Worktext. There is one worksheet for all three levels, but learners working at different levels answer different questions. Tasks are scored by points; guidelines for assigning points are provided in the unit-specific Notes to the Teacher sections.

Writing. There are two types of tasks, one for the Photo Stories and one for the Worktext.

- Photo Stories: Learners complete a sentence by unscrambling letters to form a missing word. The scrambled words appear in the Dictionary at the end of each Photo Story episode. Tasks are scored by points, one point for each correct answer. Answer keys are provided in the unit-specific Notes to the Teacher sections.
- Worktext: This task mirrors the one in the Read and Write section of the Worktext. There is one worksheet for all three levels; learners working at different levels will respond differently, both in the amount of information and the kind of information they produce. This section is scored holistically. Scoring Guidelines are provided on pages xvi–xviii.

Critical Thinking. These tasks are for learners using the Worktext, not for learners using the Photo Stories. The questions on the learners' worksheets differ according to proficiency levels, but the scoring system is the same for all three levels. Questions are designed to assess learners' skills in expressing their ideas about the theme of each episode, ideas in the What do you Think? section of the Worktext, or ideas in the Culture Clip section of the video and Worktext. Answers are scored holistically. Scoring Guidelines are provided on page xix.

Learner Log
(Photo Stories and all levels of Worktext)

1. What words did you learn in this episode? Write them here.

   _____   _____   _____

   _____   _____   _____

   _____   _____   _____

   _____   _____   _____

   _____   _____   _____

2. What else did you learn in this episode? Write your thoughts.

   _____

   _____

   _____

   _____

   _____

   _____

3. a. Where did you use the English that you learned in this episode?

   _____

   _____

   _____

   b. How did others respond to your English?

   _____

   _____

   _____

   c. How did you feel about your ability to understand and be understood in English?

   _____

   _____

   _____

Writing Assessment

Name _____ Worktext Unit _____ Date _____

_____

_____

_____

_____

_____

_____

_____

_____

_____

_____

_____

_____

_____

_____

_____

_____

_____

_____

_____

_____

_____

_____

_____

Score Sheet

Name _____ Unit _____ Date _____

Skill Area	Proficiency Level			
	Photo Story	✪	✪✪	✪✪✪
Listening	___ of 4	___ of 5	___ of 5	___ of 5
Speaking	___ of 4	___ of 5	___ of 5	___ of 5
Language Structure		___ of 5	___ of 5	___ of 5
Reading	___ of 4	___ of 5	___ of 5	___ of 5
Writing	___ of 4	___ of 5	___ of 5	___ of 5
Critical Thinking		___ of 5	___ of 5	___ of 5
Total	___ of 16	___ of 30	___ of 30	___ of 30
Percentage	# points × $6\frac{1}{4}$ = %	# points × $3\frac{1}{3}$ = %	# points × $3\frac{1}{3}$ = %	# points × $3\frac{1}{3}$ = %

Interpretation of Scores

Photo Stories

Score	Percent	Interpretation
15–16	94–100%	may be ready to try next level
13–14	81–93%	doing well
11–12	69–80%	doing average
0–10	0–68%	may need additional help

Worktext

Score	Percent	Interpretation
29–30	96–100%	ready for next level
24–28	80–95%	doing well
20–23	66–79%	doing average
0–19	0–65%	performing below level
		(move down a level if possible)

Guidelines for Holistic Scoring

Speaking: Photo Stories

Score	Pronunciation	Responses/Communication	Vocabulary/Structure
4	readily understandable	appropriate and always relate to question	comprehensible and grammatically correct
3	usually understandable occassional errors that interfere with meaning	appropriate and usually relate to question	comprehensible, but not grammatically correct
2	errors often interfere with meaning	often not appropriate and do not always relate to question	often not comprehensible and grammatical errors interfere with meaning
1	errors always interfere with meaning and often incomprehensible	inappropriate response and meaning unclear	incomprehensible and inappropriate

Crossroads Café Assessment A

Speaking: ✪

Score	Pronunciation (including stress and intonation)	Responses (in words and phrases)	Vocabulary and Common Expressions
5	readily understandable	always appropriate and relate to the question	used appropriately and correctly
4	usually understandable	usually appropriate and relate to the question	usually used appropriately and correctly
3	errors sometimes interfere with understanding	sometimes inappropriate or not related to the question, but meaning is clear	may be used inappropriately or incorrectly, but meaning is clear
2	errors often interfere with understanding	frequently inappropriate and so unrelated to question that understanding meaning is difficult	often used inappropriately or incorrectly, which interferes with meaning
1	errors always interfere with understanding	unrelated to question, and meaning is unclear	used inappropriately or incorrectly; meaning is unclear

Speaking: ✪✪

Score	Pronunciation (including stress and intonation)	Responses (in sentences)	Vocabulary and Common Expressions
5	readily understandable	ideas expressed clearly and supported with examples; no grammatical errors	used appropriately and correctly
4	usually understandable	ideas usually expressed clearly and supported with examples; few grammatical errors	usually used appropriately and correctly
3	errors sometimes interfere with understanding	ideas not always expressed clearly or supported with examples; many grammatical errors but most do not interfere with meaning	may be used inappropriately or incorrectly, but meaning is clear
2	errors often interfere with understanding	ideas frequently not expressed clearly or supported with examples; so many grammatical errors that understanding meaning is difficult	often used inappropriately or incorrectly, which interferes with meaning
1	errors always interfere with understanding	ideas not expressed clearly and not supported with examples; so many grammatical errors that meaning is unclear	used inappropriately or incorrectly; meaning is unclear

Speaking: ✪✪✪

Score	Pronunciation (including stress and intonation)	Responses (in sentences)	Usage: Sentence Structure, Verb Forms, Grammar	Vocabulary and Common Expressions
5	readily understandable	ideas expressed clearly and supported with examples; sentences flow (relate to each other)	used correctly	used appropriately and correctly
4	usually understandable	ideas usually expressed clearly and supported with examples; most sentences flow (relate to each other)	few errors	usually used appropriately and correctly
3	errors sometimes interfere with understanding	ideas not always expressed clearly or supported with examples; some sentences do not flow (do not relate to each other)	complex sentences and complex verb forms, when used, may be incorrect; many grammatical errors, but most do not interfere with meaning	may be used inappropriately or incorrectly, but meaning is clear
2	errors often interfere with understanding	ideas frequently not expressed clearly, not supported with examples, and do not relate to each other	so many errors that understanding meaning is difficult	often used inappropriately or incorrectly, which interferes with meaning
1	errors always interfere with understanding	ideas not expressed clearly, not supported with examples, and do not relate to each other	so many errors that meaning is unclear	used inappropriately or incorrectly; meaning is unclear

Language Structure ✪

Score	Responses (in words and phrases)
5	always appropriate for the question
4	usually appropriate for the question
3	sometimes appropriate for the question
2	frequently inappropriate for the question
1	always inappropriate for the question

Language Structure ✪✪

Score	Responses (in sentences)
5	almost always appropriate for question
4	usually appropriate for question
3	sometimes appropriate for question
2	frequently inappropriate for the question
1	always inappropriate for the question

Language Structure ✪✪✪

Score	Responses (in sentences)
5	almost always appropriate for the question and grammatically correct
4	usually appropriate for the question and grammatically correct
3	sometimes appropriate for the question and grammatically correct
2	frequently inappropriate for the question and grammatically incorrect
1	always inappropriate for the question and grammatically incorrect

Writing: ✪

Score	Ideas	Mechanics: Capitalization, Punctuation, Grammar	Vocabulary and Common Expressions
5	produces simple sentences related to topic	used correctly	used appropriately and correctly
4	produces simple sentences, most relating to the topic	usually correct	usually used appropriately and correctly
3	produces simple sentences, but several do not relate to the topic	errors sometimes interfere with meaning	may be used inappropriately or incorrectly, but meaning is clear
2	ideas frequently do not relate to topic	so many errors that understanding meaning is difficult	often used inappropriately or incorrectly, which interferes with meaning
1	ideas do not relate to one another	so many errors that meaning is unclear	used inappropriately or incorrectly; meaning is unclear

Score	Ideas	Mechanics: Capitalization, Punctuation, Grammar	Vocabulary and Common Expressions
5	produces sentences that flow and relate to one another	ideas consistently expressed in complete sentences; capitalization, punctuation and grammar used correctly	used appropriately and correctly
4	produces sentences that flow and most sentences relate to one another	ideas usually expressed in complete sentences; capitalization and punctuation usually correct; few grammatical errors	usually used appropriately and correctly
3	produces sentences but several do not relate to the topic	ideas not always expressed in complete sentences; many grammatical errors, but most do not interfere with meaning	may be used inappropriately or incorrectly, but meaning is clear
2	ideas frequently do not relate to the topic	ideas frequently not expressed in complete sentences; so many grammatical errors that understanding meaning is difficult	often used inappropriately or incorrectly, which interferes with meaning
1	ideas do not relate to one another	ideas not expressed in complete sentences; so many grammatical errors that meaning is unclear	used inappropriately or incorrectly; meaning is unclear

Writing: ✪✪✪

Score	Ideas	Mechanics: Capitalization, Punctuation, Grammar	Vocabulary and Common Expressions
5	well-developed paragraph: main idea clear and several supporting pieces of information	ideas expressed in complete sentences; capitalization and punctuation consistently correct; complex sentences, complex verb forms, and grammar used correctly	used appropriately and correctly
4	well-developed paragraph: states main idea and provides some supporting details	ideas expressed in complete sentences; capitalization and punctuation usually correct; complex sentences and complex verb forms usually used correctly; few grammatical errors	usually used appropriately and correctly
3	paragraph with main idea and some supporting details, but not all details relate to main idea	ideas not always expressed in complete sentences; complex sentences and complex verb forms, when used, may be incorrect; some grammatical errors but most do not interfere with meaning	may be used inappropriately or incorrectly, but meaning is clear
2	ideas may not be in paragraph form and frequently do not relate to main idea or to one another	ideas frequently not expressed in complete sentences; so many errors in sentence structure, verb forms, and grammar that understanding meaning is difficult	often used inappropriately or incorrectly, which interferes with meaning
1	writing does not identify main idea; ideas do not relate to a main idea or to one another	ideas not expressed in complete sentences; errors in sentence structure, verb forms, and/or grammar obscure meaning	used inappropriately or incorrectly; meaning is unclear

Critical Thinking (all levels)

5	states ideas clearly and supports them with details; demonstrates ability to analyze, synthesize, and evaluate
4	states ideas clearly and provides some supporting details; some analysis, synthesis, and evaluation
3	ideas not always clear, and not all details support the ideas; some analysis, synthesis, or evaluation
2	ideas seldom clear; few or no supporting details; little analysis, synthesis, or evaluation
1	ideas not clear and no supporting details; no analysis, synthesis, or evaluation

Name _____ Date _____

Listening Look at each picture. Listen to the tape. Write the letter of the correct picture on the line.

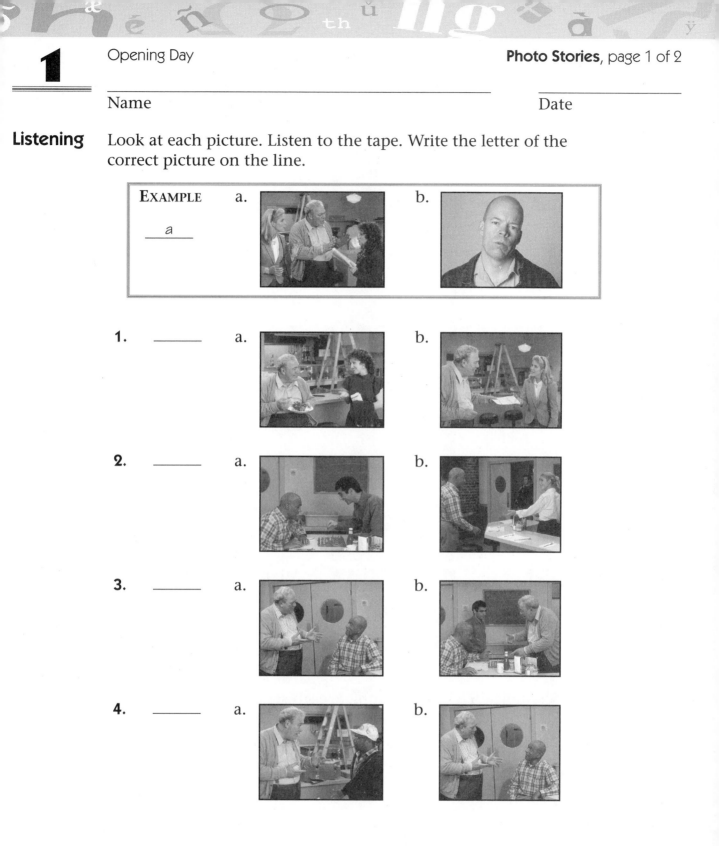

EXAMPLE a. b.

_a_

1. _____ a. b.

2. _____ a. b.

3. _____ a. b.

4. _____ a. b.

Speaking Who works at Crossroads Café? What are their jobs? Think about your answers. Tell as much as you can. Your teacher will listen.

Reading   Look at each picture. Choose a, b, or c. Write the letter on the line.

EXAMPLE

_____a_____

Rosa and Katherine want
a. an interview.
b. a résumé.
c. a menu.

---

1. _____

Rosa wants
a. to deliver food.
b. to cook.
c. to be a waitress.

2. _____

Rosa gives Mr. Brashov
a. a dessert.
b. an application.
c. an interview.

3. _____

Mr. Brashov gives Henry
a. a menu.
b. a hamburger.
c. directions.

4. _____

Mr. Brashov and Jess
a. order coffee.
b. play chess.
c. apply for a job.

Writing   Unscramble each word. Complete each sentence.

EXAMPLE   Rosa was late for her job

i n t e r v i e w.
(n e v r t i e w i)

---

1. The cook ___ ___ ___ ___ the job. (u t i q)

2. Henry is a ___ ___ ___ ___ ___ ___ ___ . (e n g e a t e r)

3. Rosa has an ___ ___ ___ ___ ___ ___ ___ ___ ___ ___ ___ with
Mr. Brashov. (p o n m t i p a e n t)

4. Henry needs to ___ ___ ___ ___ ___ ___ ___ the lunch.
(e i v l d e r)

_____   _____

Name   Date

Listening   Read each question. Watch the videotape. Circle the letter of the correct answer.

> **EXAMPLE**   How does Mr. Brashov feel?
> a. excited
> b. worried _(circled)_
> c. angry

1. How do the two men feel?
   a. excited
   b. worried
   c. angry

2. What does Katherine want to talk about?
   a. her experience
   b. her weight
   c. her family

3. What is Rosa talking about?
   a. her country
   b. her problems
   c. her last job

4. What is Henry going to deliver for Mr. Brashov?
   a. some food
   b. some money
   c. a package

5. How does Jamal feel about his job in the restaurant?
   a. lucky
   b. worried
   c. disappointed

Speaking   Talk about this picture. Tell as much as you can. Your teacher will listen.

Language Structure   Give personal information.

> EXAMPLE
>
>
> Excuse me, young man. What is your name?
>
> What is your name? My name is _Henry Chang._

1. What is your name?

   My name is _____

2. Where are you from?

   I am from _____

3. Where were you born?

   I was born in _____

4. What is your teacher's name?

   Her or His name is _____

5. Where was your father born?

   He was born in _____

Critical Thinking   Think about the question below. Write your ideas. Then talk about your ideas. Your teacher will listen.

> *Do you think Katherine Blake knows the rules for a successful job interview? Tell why or why not.*

_____

_____

_____

_____

_____   _____
Name   Date

Listening   Read each question. Watch the videotape. Circle the letter of the correct answer.

EXAMPLE	Why is Mr. Brashov worried?
	a. The construction is not finished.
	b. The restaurant has no name.
	c. both a and b

1. Why is the cook angry?
   a. He wants more money.
   b. He wants better hours.
   c. He wants a better oven.

2. What does Mr. Brashov want to talk about?
   a. why Katherine is so thin
   b. where Katherine worked before
   c. how Katherine heard about the job

3. What happened to Rosa?
   a. She had a flat tire.
   b. She was in an accident.
   c. She took the wrong bus.

4. What will the customer give Henry?
   a. some food
   b. some money
   c. some trouble

5. What are Jess and Jamal talking about?
   a. Jamal's engineering job
   b. how Jamal met Mr. Brashov
   c. how Mr. Brashov met Jess

Speaking   In this episode, many people applied for jobs. Some people made good impressions and some didn't. Tell how to make a good impression during a job interview. What should you do? Tell as much as you can. Your teacher will listen.

Language Structure

Give and get personal information.

EXAMPLE	What is Katherine's last name?
	Her last name is Blake.

1. What is your first name? _____

2. What is your last name? _____

3. Where were you born? _____

4. Where are you from? _____

5. What is your friend's name? _____

Critical Thinking

Think about the question below. Write your ideas. Then talk about your ideas. Your teacher will listen.

Do you think the classified ads are a good way to find out about jobs? Tell why or why not.

_____

_____

_____

_____

_____

_____

_____

_____

_____

_____

_____

_____

_____

_____

Name _____   Date _____

Listening   Read each question. Watch the videotape. Circle the letter of the correct answer.

EXAMPLE   What can you say about the woman in the picture?
    a. She told Mr. Brashov not to open a restaurant.
    (b.) She told Mr. Brashov to open a restaurant.
    c. She gave Mr. Brashov a name for the restaurant.

---

  1. What does the cook think?
    a. The restaurant will be closed in a month.
    b. The restaurant will be open in two days.
    c. The restaurant needs two cooks.

  2. What does Katherine want to tell Mr. Brashov?
    a. that she is married
    b. that she has experience
    c. that she can cook

  3. Why didn't Rosa make a good impression?
    a. She was talking about her problems.
    b. She didn't fill out an application form.
    c. She didn't call to make an appointment.

  4. How does Henry feel?
    a. He is surprised that Mr. Brashov trusts him.
    b. He is worried that he will be late.
    c. He is upset that he got lost.

  5. How did Jamal get to know Mr. Brashov?
    a. Jamal's great uncle helped Mr. Brashov.
    b. Jamal's landlord helped Mr. Brashov.
    c. Jamal's boss helped Mr. Brashov.

Speaking   When the cook quits, he says, "This place won't even be here in a month." Do you agree with the cook? Do you think Mr. Brashov's restaurant will be open in a month? Tell as much as you can. Your teacher will listen.

Language Structure Give and get personal information.

EXAMPLE	What is Mr. Brashov's first name?
	His first name is Victor.

1. What's your name? _____

2. What's your friend's last name? _____

3. Where is your friend from? _____

4. Write a question asking your teacher her/his last name.

    _____

5. Write a question asking your teacher where she/he was born.

    _____

Critical Thinking Think about the question below. Write your ideas. Then talk about your ideas. Your teacher will listen.

Are the rules for a good job interview the same in this country as they are in your native country? Tell how they are the same or different.

_____

_____

_____

_____

_____

_____

_____

_____

_____

_____

_____   _____
Name   Date

Reading   Read the job application. Answer the questions.

JOB APPLICATION			

Name: Smith / Last   Mark / First   David / Middle

Address: 657 / Number   Fifth Ave. / Street   204 / Apt.

Lakeville / City   IL / State   61111 / Zip

Telephone: 815 / Area Code   555-6024 / Number

Social Security Number: 340-48-1234

U.S. Citizen ☑ yes ☐ no

Employment Record	Present Job	Previous Job
Job Position	cook	waiter
Company Name	Emerald Restaurant	Lou's Diner
City	Lakeville	Lakeville
Dates of Employment	From 8/85 To 9/95	From 1/80 To 8/85
Job Duties:	Present Job	Previous Job
	Cook seafood/meat; Make desserts	waiter

Person to be notified in case of emergency

Name: Beth Smith   Phone Number: (815) 555-6024
Address: 657 Fifth Ave., Lakeville, Illinois 61111

DATE: September 10, 1997   Signature: _Mark D. Smith_

✪ 1. What is his first name? _____

2. What is his last name? _____

3. Where does he live? _____

4. What is his present job? _____

5. When was his last job? _____

✪✪ 1. When did Mark leave his job at the Emerald Restaurant? _____

2. When did Mark start his job at Lou's Diner? _____

3. How much experience does Mark have? _____

4. Who is Mark's emergency contact? _____

5. What does Mark cook at the Emerald Restaurant? _____

✪✪✪ 1. Do you think Mark makes more money at the Emerald Restaurant? Why or why not? _____

_____

2. Do you think Mark is a good employee? Why or why not? _____

_____

Writing   In this unit, Katherine wrote in her diary about her new job. Now you write a diary entry for Henry about his new job.

Learner Checklist

1. Rate yourself.

I CAN . . .	ALWAYS	SOMETIMES	NEVER
get and give personal information.	❑	❑	❑
read job application forms.	❑	❑	❑
write about people.	❑	❑	❑
talk about U.S. job interview behavior.	❑	❑	❑

2. Meet with your teacher. Talk about how successful you were in reaching the goals for this unit. Compare how you rated yourself with how your teacher rated you.

3. Think about your rating and your teacher's rating. What do you need to study more?

_____

_____

_____

fold -- fold

Instructor Checklist

1. Rate the learner. For each item, circle a number based on the following scale:

   3 = easily understood, 2 = understood with difficulty, 1 = not understood

THE LEARNER CAN . . .	RATING	COMMENTS
get and give personal information.	1 2 3	
read job application forms.	1 2 3	
write about people.	1 2 3	
talk about U.S. job interview behavior.	1 2 3	

2. Meet with the learner. Use the two completed checklists to talk about learner outcomes in this unit and priorities for further study.

Opening Day

Photo Stories

— Listening Answer Key
1. b **2.** b **3.** a **4.** b

— Speaking
Either have students respond to you face to face, or have students record their responses on audiotapes. See Guidelines, page xii, for scoring.

— Reading Answer Key
1. c **2.** a **4.** c **5.** b

— Writing Answer Key
1. quit **2.** teenager **3.** appointment **4.** deliver

Worktext ✪

— Listening Answer Key
1. c **2.** a **3.** b **4.** a **5.** a

— Speaking
Either have students respond to you face to face, or have students record their responses on audiotapes. See Guidelines, page xiii, for scoring.

— Language Structure
See Guidelines, page xvi, for scoring.

— Critical Thinking
Answers will vary. See Guidelines, page xx, for scoring.

— Reading Answer Key
Each answer is worth one point.
1. David **2.** Smith **3.** Lakeville, IL, USA **4.** cook **5.** Jan. '80–Aug. '85

— Writing
Answers will vary. See Guidelines, page xvii, for scoring.

Worktext ✪✪

— Listening Answer Key
1. c **2.** a **3.** c **4.** b **5.** b

— Speaking
Either have students respond to you face to face, or have them record their responses on audiotapes. If learners are unable to respond,

• move to the one-star assessment for Speaking.

- ask more detailed questions about the episode, such as

  "What problems is Mr. Brashov having?"

  OR

  "Tell about all the new employees in the restaurant."

Variation: Ask questions about pictures in Before You Watch (page 2). For example, point to picture #3 and ask: "Who is applying for a job; point to picture #4 and ask "What is the problem?"

See Guidelines, page xiv, for scoring.

— Language Structure
See Guidelines, page xvi, for scoring.

— Critical Thinking
Answers will vary. See Guidelines, page xx, for scoring.

— Reading Answer Key
Each answer is worth one point.
1. 9/95   **2.** 1/80   **3.** 15/fifteen years   **4.** Beth Smith
5. seafood, meat, desserts

— Writing
Answers will vary. See Guidelines, page xviii, for scoring.

Worktext ✪✪✪

— Listening Answer Key
1. a   **2.** b   **3.** a   **4.** a   **5.** a

— Speaking
Either have students respond to you face to face, or have them record their responses on audiotapes. If administered face to face and learners have difficulty, do one of the following:

- move to the two-star assessment for Speaking.
- ask more detailed questions, such as the following:

  <u>for the meaning of the title</u>

  Why is this chapter called "Opening Day?"
  What new characters are introduced?
  Why is this opening day difficult?

  <u>for telling the story</u>

  How does Mr. Brashov feel about opening day?
  What problems does he have?
  What does Rosa do to get a job there?
  What does Katherine do to get a job there?
  How does the restaurant get a name?

Variation: Have learners respond to general statements such as the following:

> *Tell about Mr. Brashov's problems.*
> *Tell how Rosa and Katherine interact.*
> *Tell how Mr. Brashov gets a chef, a waitress, and a name for his restaurant.*

See Guidelines, page xv, for scoring.

Language Structure

See Guidelines, page xvi, for scoring.

Critical Thinking

Answers will vary. See Guidelines, page xx, for scoring.

Reading Answer Key

Each answer is worth two and one-half points.
Answers will vary. Possible answers:

1. Yes, because he has experience/has worked for many years; no, because it is not easy to change jobs.
2. Yes, because he always works; he was a waiter, and now he is a cook.

Writing

Answers will vary. See Guidelines, page xix, for scoring.

1

Photo Stories

| EXAMPLE | Rosa and Katherine want an interview for the job. |

1. Mr. Brashov hires Katherine.
2. Jess and Jamal play chess.
3. Mr. Brashov meets Jess.
4. Jess names the restaurant.

Worktext All Levels

| EXAMPLE | MR. BRASHOV: | Look at this place. We open in less than a week, and there is still so much to do. Cleaning, electrical work, painting . . . we don't even have a name yet. Who goes to a restaurant that has no name? Maybe tomorrow I will think of something. This restaurant is your idea, Eva. So, what do you want to call it? It would all be so much easier if you were here. |

1. MR. BRASHOV: This is not any other restaurant. This is . . .

   CHEF: a big mess. Your restaurant doesn't even have a name. Face it Brashov, you don't know what you're doing.

   MR. BRASHOV: Well, I know that I am going to open this restaurant in two days.

   CHEF: Well, I won't be here to see it. You can find yourself another cook.

   MR. BRASHOV: Fine. I will do that.

   CHEF: This place won't even be here in a month

   MR. BRASHOV: Yeah, fine. Fine. Go on, go on. Come back in a month, and we will see who is right.

2. KATHERINE: Here's my résumé. I think you'll find I've had a lot of experience especially in the area of . . .

   MR. BRASHOV: Look how thin you are. How could you work in a restaurant and be so thin?

   KATHERINE: Just lucky, I guess. It runs in the family. Anyway, the first restaurant that I worked at was . . .

   MR. BRASHOV: Have something to eat first. And then we can talk. Please.

   KATHERINE: What is this?

   MR. BRASHOV: Romanian Sausage.

   KATHERINE: Oh.

3. ROSA: I'm looking for Mr. Brashov.

MR. BRASHOV: And you have found him.

ROSA: I'm sorry I'm late. My day has been a total nightmare. First my roommate's car wouldn't start. Dead battery. So, I had to run to the bus stop and got on the bus just as it was pulling away. I was in such a hurry that I didn't read the sign on the front. You know, the little one near the top that says where the bus is going. Anyway, by the time I realized I was on the wrong bus, it was too late. So, I had to get off, find the right one and . . . anyway, here I am.

MR. BRASHOV: Who are you?

ROSA: I am Rosa Rivera. I called yesterday about the ad for the waitress job.

4. HENRY: You really want me to deliver this for you?

MR. BRASHOV: Here is the address, and here are the directions. And here is our telephone number, in case you have a problem.

HENRY: Is this some kind of joke?

MR. BRASHOV: You will do fine. Deliver the food first. Then you will take just two short blocks to the post office. The customer will give you a tip, and I will give you something for your trouble.

5. JESS: Tough break losing your job.

JAMAL: Yes, but I'm lucky I had Mr. Brashov to help me out.

JESS: So, how does an unemployed engineer end up working at a restaurant?

JAMAL: When Mr. Brashov was new in this country, my great uncle was his landlord. He helped Mr. Brashov a lot. —Very nice. Now, I am new in this country and Mr. Brashov is helping me. We're like family.

Name _____

Date _____

Listening Look at each picture. Listen to the tape. Write the letter of the correct picture on the line.

EXAMPLE   a.   b.

_a_

1. _____   a.   b.

2. _____   a.   b.

3. _____   a.   b.

4. _____   a.   b.

Speaking What is Henry's new experience? What is Mr. Brashov's new experience? Think about your answers. Tell as much as you can. Your teacher will listen.

Reading   Look at each picture. Choose a, b, or c. Write the letter on the line.

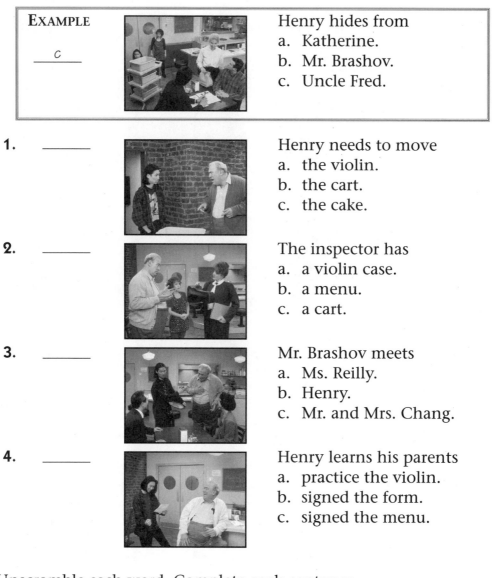

EXAMPLE

___c___

Henry hides from
a. Katherine.
b. Mr. Brashov.
c. Uncle Fred.

1. _____

Henry needs to move
a. the violin.
b. the cart.
c. the cake.

2. _____

The inspector has
a. a violin case.
b. a menu.
c. a cart.

3. _____

Mr. Brashov meets
a. Ms. Reilly.
b. Henry.
c. Mr. and Mrs. Chang.

4. _____

Henry learns his parents
a. practice the violin.
b. signed the form.
c. signed the menu.

Writing   Unscramble each word. Complete each sentence.

EXAMPLE   Henry __h__ __i__ __d__ __e__ __s__ from Uncle Fred. (i d e h s)

1. Henry wants to buy an electric ___ ___ ___ ___ ___ ___.
   (u t a g i r)

2. Ms. Reilly is an ___ ___ ___ ___ ___ ___ ___ ___ ___ looking for
   problems. (n p c t r e s i o)

3. Mr. Brashov read the ___ ___ ___ ___ ___ ___ from the inspector.
   (e p r r t o)

4. Henry told a ___ ___ ___ about the work form. (i l e)

_____   _____

Name   Date

Listening   Read each question. Watch the videotape. Circle the letter of the correct answer.

EXAMPLE   What is Ms. Reilly talking about?
                 (a.) an inspection
                 b.   a job notice
                 c.   a party

1. How does Henry feel?
    a.   happy
    b.   worried
    c.   sad

2. What does Mr. Brashov think about Henry?
    a.   He is a good worker.
    b.   He is not a good worker.
    c.   He is not important.

3. What is everyone talking about?
    a.   Henry's band
    b.   Henry's job
    c.   Henry's class

4. How does Ms. Reilly feel?
    a.   happy
    b.   sad
    c.   angry

5. How do Mr. and Mrs. Chang feel?
    a.   sad
    b.   angry
    c.   surprised

Speaking   Talk about this picture. Tell as much as you can. Your teacher will listen.

Language Structure

Make introductions.

EXAMPLE	You are Katherine Blake. Introduce yourself.
	I am Katherine Blake, the waitress at Crossroads Café.

1. You are Jess Washington. Introduce yourself. _____

   _____

2. You are Ms. Reilly. Introduce yourself. _____

   _____

3. You are Mr. Brashov. Introduce yourself. _____

   _____

4. You are Rosa. Introduce yourself. _____

   _____

5. Introduce yourself to a classmate. _____

   _____

Critical Thinking

Think about the questions below. Write your ideas. Then talk about your ideas. Your teacher will listen.

Why did Henry lie to his parents about his job? What would you tell Henry about being truthful in the future?

_____

_____

_____

_____

_____

_____

_____

_____

_____

_____

2

Name _____   Date _____

Listening   Read each question. Watch the videotape. Circle the letter of the correct answer.

EXAMPLE	How does Mr. Brashov feel about Ms. Reilly's visit?
	a. He is angry.
	(b.) He is surprised.
	c. He is sad.

1. What are Rosa and Henry talking about?
   a. why Henry is going to school
   b. why his uncle came to the restaurant
   c. why Henry is hiding

2. Henry left the bussing cart in the wrong place. What does Mr. Brashov think?
   a. It is important.
   b. It is unimportant.
   c. It is the end of the world.

3. What does Mrs. Chang think about Henry's job?
   a. It will lead to something better.
   b. It won't help him play the violin better.
   c. It won't lead to something better.

4. What happened to Ms. Reilly?
   a. She tripped over a violin case.
   b. She violated a rule.
   c. She wrote her report.

5. What do Mr. and Mrs. Chang think about Henry's violin practice?
   a. They think Henry likes to play the violin.
   b. They think Henry only likes to earn money.
   c. They think Henry only likes to study.

Speaking   This episode was about learning experiences. Mr. Brashov learned about the restaurant business, and Henry learned about talking to his parents and telling the truth. Sometimes it is difficult to learn new things. Think about an experience you had growing up. What did you learn? Was it difficult or easy? Tell as much as you can. Your teacher will listen.

Language Structure Make introductions and respond to introductions.

EXAMPLE	You are Katherine Blake. Introduce yourself to Mrs. Chang.
	I'm Katherine Blake, the waitress.
	How does Mrs. Chang respond?
	It's a pleasure to meet you.

1. Introduce Ms. Reilly to Jamal. _____

_____

2. You are Henry. Introduce Jamal to your parents. _____

_____

3. Mr. Brashov introduces Rosa to Ms. Reilly. Ms. Reilly says, "It's nice to meet you." How does Rosa respond to Ms. Reilly?

_____

4. Henry's Uncle Fred is glad to meet Mr. Brashov. What does Uncle Fred say to Mr. Brashov?

_____

5. Introduce Jess Washington to Henry's parents, Mr. and Mrs. Chang.

_____

Critical Thinking Think about the question below. Write your ideas. Then talk about your ideas. Your teacher will listen.

Do you think it's a good idea or a bad idea for high school students to work? Tell why or why not. Give examples to support your opinion.

_____

_____

_____

_____

_____

_____ _____
Name   Date

Listening   Read each question. Watch the videotape. Circle the letter of the correct answer.

EXAMPLE	What does Ms. Reilly expect to find at the café?
	(a.) She will probably find some problems.
	b. She will probably not find any problems.
	c. She will never find any problems.

1. What does Rosa tell Henry?
   a. that his parents should know the truth
   b. that his uncle should know the truth
   c. that his parents should not know the truth

2. How does Henry feel after his talk with Mr. Brashov?
   a. angry
   b. sad
   c. confused

3. What does Henry want to buy?
   a. things for himself
   b. things for his family
   c. things for his friends

4. What will Mr. Brashov do?
   a. report the violin case accident
   b. write about the violin case in the report
   c. find out about the violin case

5. What does Henry tell his parents?
   a. He doesn't want to practice the violin.
   b. He wants to practice the violin.
   c. He never wants to practice the violin.

Speaking   Explain the title, "Growing Pains," or tell the story. Tell as much as you can. Your teacher will listen.

Language Structure   Make introductions and respond to introductions.

> | EXAMPLE | You are Katherine Blake. Introduce yourself to Ms. Reilly. |
> |---|---|
> | | I'm Katherine Blake, the waitress at Crossroads Café. |
> | | How does Ms. Reilly respond? |
> | | It's a pleasure to meet you. OR Glad to meet you. |

1. Introduce Rosa to Ms. Reilly. _____

   _____

   _____

2. Henry introduces Jess Washington to his parents. _____

   _____

   _____

3. Henry's Uncle Fred and Mr. Brashov are happy to meet each other. What do they say to each other?

   Mr. Brashov: _____

   _____

   Uncle Fred: _____

   _____

Critical Thinking   Think about the question below. Write your ideas. Then talk about your ideas. Your teacher will listen.

> *Do you think it's easier to tell the truth than to lie? Tell why or why not.*

_____

_____

_____

_____

_____

_____

_____

_____ _____

Name   Date

Reading   Read the field trip permission form. Answer the questions.

My son/(daughter) Sara Grayson has permission to attend the field trip to the Crown Theater on December 12, 1997. The purpose of the trip is to see the stage production of Scrooge. The bus will leave Middletown High School at 12:30 P.M. and return at 7:00 P.M.. The cost of the trip is $15.00. The money is due on December 5, 1997. Additional spending money is needed/(not needed). My son/(daughter) has read the field trip rules on the reverse side and agrees to follow them.

Emily Grayson   12/5/97   *Sara Grayson*   12/5/97

(parent's signature)   date   (student's signature)   date

✪ 1. When is the field trip? _____

     2. What time does the field trip begin? _____

     3. What time does it end? _____

     4. How much does it cost? _____

     5. When did the parent sign the form? _____

✪✪ 1. Who signed the form? _____

     2. Where are the students going? _____

     3. What are the students going to see? _____

     4. Where does the bus leave from? _____

     5. How much extra money do the students need? _____

✪✪✪ 1. Why are the students going on a field trip? _____

                 _____

     2. Who is sponsoring the trip? _____

     3. Who is paying for the trip? _____

     4. Where are the field trip rules? _____

     5. Why do you think this form is needed? _____

Writing   In this unit, Henry wrote a newspaper article about the work-study program. Now you write an article about field trips. Are they important? Tell why or why not.

Learner Checklist

1. Rate yourself.

I CAN . . .	ALWAYS	SOMETIMES	NEVER
introduce myself and others.	❏	❏	❏
read school-related forms.	❏	❏	❏
rewrite a newspaper article.	❏	❏	❏
talk about immigrants in a new culture.	❏	❏	❏

2. Meet with your teacher. Talk about how successful you were in reaching the goals for this unit. Compare how you rated yourself with how your teacher rated you.

3. Think about your rating and your teacher's rating. What do you need to study more?

_____

_____

_____

fold --- fold

Instructor Checklist

1. Rate the learner. For each item, circle a number based on the following scale:

   3 = easily understood, 2 = understood with difficulty, 1 = not understood

THE LEARNER CAN . . .	RATING	COMMENTS
introduce himself and others.	1 2 3	
read school-related forms.	1 2 3	
rewrite a newspaper article.	1 2 3	
talk about immigrants in a new culture.	1 2 3	

2. Meet with the learner. Use the two completed checklists to talk about learner outcomes in this unit and priorities for further study.

Photo Stories

— Listening Answer Key
1. a   **2.** b   **3.** b   **4.** a

— Speaking
Either have students respond to you face to face, or have students record their responses on audiotapes. See Guidelines, page xii, for scoring.

— Reading Answer Key
1. b   **2.** a   **3.** c   **4.** b

— Writing Answer Key
1. guitar   **2.** inspector   **3.** report   **4.** lie

Worktext ✪

— Listening Answer Key
1. b   **2.** a   **3.** b   **4.** c   **5.** c

— Speaking
Either have students respond to you face to face, or have students record their responses on audiotapes. See Guidelines, page xiii, for scoring.

— Language Structure
See Guidelines, page x, for scoring.
1. I am Jess Washington, a customer (or a friend of Henry).
2. I am Ms. Reilly, the health inspector.
3. I am Victor Brashov, the owner of Crossroads Café.
4. I am Rosa, the cook.
5. I am <u>student's name</u>, (first OR full), a student.

— Critical Thinking
Answers will vary. See Guidelines, page xx, for scoring.

— Reading Answer Key
Each answer is worth one point.
1. 12/12/97
2. 12:30 P.M.
3. 7:00 P.M.
4. $15.00
5. 12/5/97

— Writing
Answers will vary. See Guidelines, page xvii, for scoring.

Worktext ✪✪

— Listening Answer Key
1. c   **2.** b   **3.** c   **4.** a   **5.** b

— Speaking
Either have students respond to you face to face, or have them record their responses on audiotapes. If learners are unable to respond, do one of the following:

- move to the one-star assessment for Speaking.
- ask more detailed questions about the episode.

See Guidelines, page xiv, for scoring.

— Language Structure
See Guidelines, page xvi, for scoring.
1. Jamal, this is Ms. Reilly, the health inspector. Ms. Reilly, this is Jamal, the handyman.
2. Jamal, these are my parents, Mr. and Mrs. Chang. Mom and Dad, this is Jamal, the handyman.
3. It's nice to meet you, too.
4. I'm glad to meet you.
5. Jess, this is Mr. and Mrs. Chang, Henry's parents. Mr. and Mrs. Chang, this is Jess Washington, a customer.

— Critical Thinking
Answers will vary. See Guidelines, page xx, for scoring.

— Reading Answer Key
Each answer is worth one point.
1. Emily Grayson and Sara Grayson
2. to the Crown Theater
3. *Scrooge*
4. Middletown High School
5. none

— Writing
Answers will vary. See Guidelines, page xviii, for scoring.

Worktext ✪✪✪

— Listening Answer Key
1. a   **2.** c   **3.** a   **4.** c   **5.** b

— Speaking
Either have students respond to you face to face, or have them record their responses on audiotapes. If administered face to face and learners have difficulty, do one of the following:

- move to the two-star assessment for Speaking.

- ask more detailed questions, such as the following:

  <u>for the meaning of the title</u>
  Who had a painful experience?
  How does Henry feel about his parents?
  How does Mr. Brashov feel about having his restaurant inspected?
  Was it easy for Henry to talk to his parents?

  <u>for telling the story</u>
  Why does Henry lie to his parents?
  Why does Henry hide from his uncle?
  Why is Mr. Brashov nervous?
  What do the workers think about Ms. Reilly's visit?
  What does Henry learn about telling the truth?
  What do Mr. and Mrs. Chang learn about Henry?

Variation: Have learners respond to general statements such as the following:

  Tell about Ms. Reilly's inspection.
  Tell about the birthday party.
  Tell about Henry and his parents.
  Tell what Mr. Brashov thinks about Ms. Reilly's inspection.

See Guidelines, page xv, for scoring.

Language Structure
See Guidelines, page xvi, for scoring.
1. Ms. Reilly, this is Rosa, the cook at Crossroads Café. Rosa, this is Ms. Reilly, the health inspector.
2. Jess, these are my parents, Mr. and Mrs. Chang. Mom and Dad, this is Jess Washington, a customer.
3. Mr. Brashov: It's a pleasure to meet you. OR It's nice to meet you. OR Glad to meet you. Uncle Fred: It's a pleasure to meet you, too. OR It's nice to meet you, too. OR Glad to meet you, too.

Critical Thinking
Answers will vary. See Guidelines, page xx, for scoring.

Reading Answer Key
Each answer is worth one point.
1. to see a stage production of *Scrooge*
2. Middletown High School
3. the parent or the student
4. on the reverse of the form
5. so the parents know about the trip; so the parents make arrangements to pick up their children at 7:00 P.M.; so the students behave.

Writing
Answers will vary. See Guidelines, page xix, for scoring.

Photo Stories

EXAMPLE	Henry hides from Uncle Fred.

1. Mr. Brashov meets Uncle Fred.
2. Uncle Fred arrives at the party.
3. Mr. and Mrs. Chang look at the signatures.
4. Mr. Brashov gets the inspector's report.

Worktext All Levels

EXAMPLE	MR. BRASHOV:	Are you here for lunch?
	MS. REILLY:	No, I'm here to inspect the restaurant.
	MR. BRASHOV:	For what?
	MS. REILLY:	Whatever I can see. And what I can't see . . . I'll find. Even very small violations that no one else would notice.
	MR. BRASHOV:	Well, no one told me you were coming.
	MS. REILLY:	It's an inspection, Mr. Brashov, not a party.

1. ROSA: Henry, what's going on?

   HENRY: The man at the table is my uncle.

   ROSA: So what's wrong with that?

   HENRY: If he sees me working here, he'll tell my parents.

   ROSA: You're not making any sense.

   HENRY: Well, my parents don't exactly know that I'm working here.

   ROSA: They don't exactly know?

   HENRY: I just didn't exactly mention that I work here. They think I'm in school every day until three o'clock.

   ROSA: Oh, Henry . . .

   HENRY: What's the big deal? I mean lots of kids do it. School in the morning—work in the afternoon.

   ROSA: The big deal is, you didn't tell your parents.

2. MR. BRASHOV: Everyone makes mistakes now and then.

   HENRY: Well, this was a pretty big mistake, and if my parents find out . . .

   MR. BRASHOV: Henry, please. You don't think I would tell your parents about something so unimportant?

   HENRY: You really won't say anything?

   MR. BRASHOV: Not a word. Leaving a bussing cart in the wrong place is not the end of the world.

   HENRY: A bussing cart? . . . uh . . . but . . . What . . .

   MR. BRASHOV: But nothing! What's important is you are doing a good job. You are responsible, dependable, and trustworthy.

3. HENRY: I go to class in the morning and work in the afternoon. The school says it's okay.

   MRS. CHANG: But your parents do not.

   MR. CHANG: And why is working so important, Henry?

   HENRY: I don't want to have to ask you for everything. I want to buy things for myself.

   MRS. CHANG: What kinds of things?

   HENRY: Like an electric guitar.

   MR. CHANG: But you play the violin.

   HENRY: Yeah, but I also want to play the guitar. I'm going to be in a band.

   MRS. CHANG: If we were still in China we wouldn't even have to talk about this.

   HENRY: But this isn't China. This is America. This is our home now.

   MR. CHANG: No, this is where we <u>live</u>. A home is a place where children respect their parents and their grandparents.

   GRANDPA CHANG: (in Chinese) Where's the dictionary? We are missing too much.

   MRS. CHANG: Going to school and learning . . . that will lead to something. Electric guitars will not. Cleaning dishes will not.

4. **MS. REILLY:** Mr. Brashov, what is this?

   MR. BRASHOV: Uh . . . it looks like a violin case.

   MS. REILLY: Obviously, it is a violin case. But the question is, what is it doing in the kitchen?

   MR. BRASHOV: Maybe one of our customers left it here accidentally. Does this violate any rules?

   MS. REILLY: Not unless someone trips over it and nearly breaks her leg.

   MR. BRASHOV: I don't know how it got there. I'll look into it right away.

   MS. REILLY: See that you do. Otherwise, you can expect to read about this little incident in my report.

   MR. BRASHOV: All right, Ms. Reilly.

5. **HENRY:** Mr. Brashov? I'm really sorry about the violin case. I have a lesson later today. I was going to practice after work.

   MR. BRASHOV: It's all right. Don't worry about it.

   MR. CHANG: Henry, you're still practicing your violin?

   HENRY: Sure. Why not?

   MR. CHANG: Well, we thought you were not interested in doing anything, but earning money.

   HENRY: I never said that.

3

Name _____ Date _____

Listening Look at each picture. Listen to the tape. Write the letter of the correct picture on the line.

EXAMPLE   a.   b.

___a___

1. _____   a.   b.

2. _____   a.   b.

3. _____   a.   b.

4. _____   a.   b.

Speaking How are Rosa and Miguel different? Think about your answer. Tell as much as you can. Your teacher will listen.

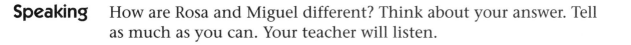

Reading   Look at each picture. Choose a, b, or c. Write the letter on the line.

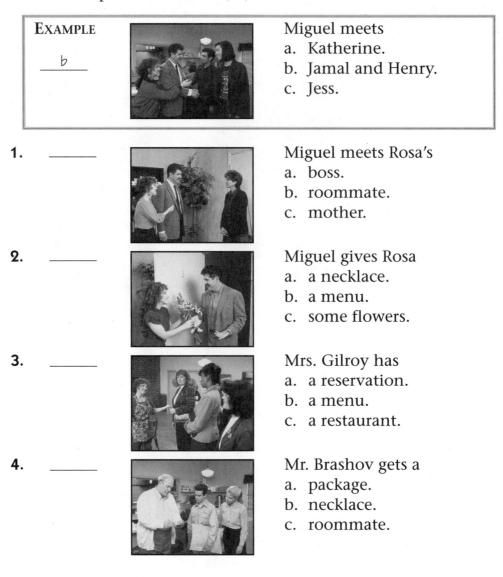

EXAMPLE		Miguel meets
_b_		a. Katherine.
		b. Jamal and Henry.
		c. Jess.

1. _____   Miguel meets Rosa's
   a. boss.
   b. roommate.
   c. mother.

2. _____   Miguel gives Rosa
   a. a necklace.
   b. a menu.
   c. some flowers.

3. _____   Mrs. Gilroy has
   a. a reservation.
   b. a menu.
   c. a restaurant.

4. _____   Mr. Brashov gets a
   a. package.
   b. necklace.
   c. roommate.

Writing   Unscramble each word. Complete each sentence.

> EXAMPLE   Miguel __m__ __e__ __e__ __t__ __s__ Jamal and Henry.
> (e e m t s)

1. Rosa can ___ ___ ___ ___ ___ ___ the restaurant. (a n g e a m)

2. The ___ ___ ___ ___ ___ ___ ___ are beautiful. (l w r s e o f)

3. Rosa wants a ___ ___ ___ ___ ___ ___ ___ ___ ___ ___ restaurant. (u c s f l u s e c s)

4. Mrs. Gilroy made a ___ ___ ___ ___ ___ ___ ___ ___ ___ ___ ___ for lunch. (e e v t o n i a r s r)

Name _____ Date _____

Listening Read each question. Watch the videotape. Circle the letter of the correct answer.

EXAMPLE What do the customers think?
    (a.) The cook quit.
    b. The waitress quit.
    c. The owner quit.

1. What does Miguel ask Rosa?
  a. to cook dinner
  b. to get married
  c. to have children

2. Who is Carrie?
  a. Rosa's sister
  b. Rosa's roommate
  c. Rosa's neighbor

3. Where does Miguel want to live?
  a. in the United States
  b. in Mexico
  c. in another country

4. What is Rosa talking about?
  a. wedding plans
  b. dinner plans
  c. restaurant plans

5. How does Miguel feel?
  a. relieved
  b. disappointed
  c. angry

Speaking Talk about this picture. Tell as much as you can. Your teacher will listen.

Language Structure Talk about wants.

EXAMPLE	What does Rosa want to do?
	She wants to <u>open a restaurant.</u>

1. Where does Miguel want to live?

   He wants to _____

2. What does Miguel want to give Rosa?

   He wants to _____

3. What does Mr. Brashov's brother want to do?

   He wants to _____

4. What do you want to buy?

   I want to _____

5. What do you want to do next year?

   I want to _____

Critical Thinking Think about the question below. Write you ideas. Then talk about your ideas. Your teacher will listen.

Do you think Rosa and Miguel are "Worlds Apart?" Tell why or why not.

_____

_____

_____

_____

_____

_____

_____

_____

_____

_____

_____

Name _____   Date _____

Listening   Read each question. Watch the videotape. Circle the letter of the correct answer.

EXAMPLE   How do the customers feel about Rosa coming back?
a. They are disappointed.
(b.) They are relieved.
c. They are sad.

---

1. Where is Miguel going to stay?
   a. at Rosa's apartment
   b. at a friend's house
   c. at a hotel

2. How does Rosa feel?
   a. She is tired.
   b. She is confused.
   c. She is angry.

3. What are Rosa and Miguel discussing?
   a. where to open a restaurant
   b. when to open a restaurant
   c. how to open a restaurant

4. What does Miguel think of Rosa's ideas?
   a. They won't be successful in Puebla.
   b. They won't be successful in the United States.
   c. They won't be successful anywhere.

5. What does Rosa tell Miguel?
   a. She wants to get married.
   b. She doesn't want to get married.
   c. She wants to think some more.

Speaking   In this episode, Rosa has to decide if she wants to return to Mexico. She has reasons to go back to her country, and she has reasons to stay in the United States. Do you think you will return to your native country to live? Give some reasons for staying in the United States. Give some reasons for going back to your native country to live. Tell as much as you can. Your teacher will listen.

Language Structure Talk about wants.

EXAMPLE	What does Miguel want?
	He wants to marry Rosa.

1. Where does Rosa want to live? _____

_____

2. What do you want? _____

_____

3. What do you want to do? _____

_____

4. Where do you want to go for dinner? _____

_____

5. When do you want to go? _____

_____

Critical Thinking Think about the question below. Write your ideas. Then talk about your ideas. Your teacher will listen.

Are your reasons for staying in the United States the same as or different from Rosa's reasons? Tell how they are the same or different.

_____

_____

_____

_____

_____

_____

_____

_____

©Heinle & Heinle Publishers
Duplication for classroom use is permitted.

3

Name _____   Date _____

Listening   Read each question. Watch the videotape. Circle the letter of the correct answer.

EXAMPLE	What do the customers think of Rosa's cooking?
	(a.) They prefer her cooking.
	b. They don't like her cooking.
	c. They don't know how she cooks.

1. What are Carrie and Rosa discussing?
   a. what Miguel will do at the conference
   b. who will stay at the apartment
   c. what Carrie will do on her date

2. How does Rosa feel about getting married?
   a. She wants to get married as soon as possible.
   b. She wants to keep studying and working.
   c. She never wants to get married.

3. What can you say about Rosa and Miguel?
   a. They have the same future plans.
   b. They have different future plans.
   c. They have no future plans.

4. What is Miguel's advice to Rosa?
   a. She should learn to be a better chef.
   b. She should take more business classes.
   c. She should think like a Mexican.

5. Why can't Rosa return to Mexico?
   a. She is a different person now.
   b. She is angry about the restaurant.
   c. She doesn't love Miguel anymore.

Speaking   Explain the title, "Worlds Apart," or tell the story. Tell as much as you can. Your teacher will listen.

Language Structure Talk about wants.

EXAMPLE	What does Rosa decide about Miguel?
	She doesn't want to marry him.

1. Why do you want to live in the United States? _____

    _____

2. Why do you want to learn English? _____

    _____

3. What does your family want to buy? _____

    _____

4. Write a question asking your teacher about wants. _____

    _____

5. Write a question asking your friend about his/her goals. _____

    _____

Critical Thinking Think about the question below. Write your ideas. Then talk about your ideas. Your teacher will listen.

Do you think all immigrants come to the United States for the same reason? Tell why or why not.

_____

_____

_____

_____

_____

_____

_____

_____

_____

Name _____ Date _____

Reading Read the pages from the Yellow Pages. Answer the questions.

	SCHOOLS 1412

Academy of Art
  Call for a free catalogue
  332 S.Michigan Ave. 461-0600
Business/East-West University
  816 S. Michigan Ave. 939-0111
Computer Discovery Center
  Convenient 6 Hr Classes/Eve & Wkds
  2940 Lincoln 348-8120
English Language School
  100 W. Adams 782-4000
Fashion Academy
  B.A. & Assoc. Degree
  1 N. State 541-3900
Travel Education Center
  Toll Free 800 945-2220
	▶ **Cooking and Hospitality**
	Institute of Chicago Inc ─────
	Associate Degree in Culinary Arts
	And Certificate Programs in
	Professional Cooking,
	Baking, Restaurant Management
	361 W. Chestnut 944-2725
	
	CULINARY SCHOOL OF KENDALL COLLEGE
	Degree Programs in Culinary Arts
	and Hospitality Management
	2408 Orrington Ave.
	Evanston 847-866-1300

✪ **1.** What is the telephone number of the English Language School?

_____

2. What is the address of the Fashion Academy? _____

3. Where is the Culinary School of Kendall College? _____

4. What is the telephone number of the Academy of Art? _____

5. What is the address of the Computer Discovery Center? _____

✪✪ **1.** Which school has an 800 number? _____

2. What kind of degrees does the Fashion Academy offer? _____

3. How many hours are the classes at the Computer Discovery

Center? _____

4. Which school offers a free catalogue? _____

✪✪✪ **1.** Do you think there are good jobs in the restaurant business? Why

or why not? _____

_____

2. Why do you think the Computer Discovery Center offers evening

and weekend classes? _____

_____

Writing In this unit, Rosa wrote a letter to Flora. Write a letter to a friend
in your country. Tell about your English class.

Learner Checklist

1. Rate yourself.

I CAN . . .	ALWAYS	SOMETIMES	NEVER
talk about things I want or want to do.	❏	❏	❏
read the yellow pages of a telephone directory.	❏	❏	❏
write a letter.	❏	❏	❏
talk about United States immigration.	❏	❏	❏

2. Meet with your teacher. Talk about how successful you were in reaching the goals for this unit. Compare how you rated yourself with how your teacher rated you.

3. Think about your rating and your teacher's rating. What do you need to study more?

_____

_____

_____

fold --- fold

Instructor Checklist

1. Rate the learner. For each item, circle a number based on the following scale.

3 = easily understood, 2 = understood with difficulty, 1 = not understood

THE LEARNER CAN . . .	RATING	COMMENTS
talk about things he or she wants or wants to do.	1 2 3	
read the yellow pages of a telephone directory.	1 2 3	
write a letter.	1 2 3	
talk about United States immigration.	1 2 3	

2. Meet with the learner. Use the two completed checklists to talk about learner outcomes in this unit and priorities for further study.

Photo Stories

— Listening Answer Key

1. a   **2.** a   **3.** b   **4.** b

— Speaking

Either have students respond to you face to face, or have students record their responses on audiotapes. See Guidelines, page xii, for scoring.

— Reading Answer Key

1. b   **2.** c   **3.** a   **4.** a

— Writing Answer Key

1. manage   **2.** flowers   **3.** successful   **4.** reservation

Worktext ✪

— Listening Answer Key

1. b   **2.** b   **3.** b   **4.** c   **5.** b

— Speaking

Either have students respond to you face to face, or have students record their responses on audiotapes. See Guidelines, page xiii, for scoring.

— Language Structure

See Guidelines, page xvi, for scoring.

1. Mexico
2. his grandmother's necklace
3. send a pillow
4. Answers will vary.
5. Answers will vary.

— Critical Thinking

Answers will vary. See Guidelines, page xx, for scoring.

— Reading Answer Key

Answers 1, 3, and 4 are worth one point each; answer 2 is worth two points.

1. 782-4000   **2.** 1 N. State   **3.** Evanston   **4.** 461-0600   **5.** 2940 Lincoln

— Writing

Answers will vary. See Guidelines, page xvii, for scoring.

Worktext ✪✪

— Listening Answer Key

1. c   **2.** b   **3.** a   **4.** a   **5.** b

Speaking

Either have students respond to you face to face, or have them record their responses on audiotapes. If learners are unable to respond, do one of the following:

- move to the one-star assessment for Speaking.
- ask more specific questions about the episode, such as

  "Tell me what happened when Miguel asked Rosa to marry him."
  OR
  "Tell me what happened when Rosa showed Miguel her plans for a restaurant."

Variation: Ask questions about pictures 1–6 in Before You Watch (p. 30). For example, point to picture #5 and ask: "What are Rosa and Miguel doing?" "What are they saying?" "How do they feel?"
See Guidelines, page xiv, for scoring.

Language Structure

See Guidelines, page xvi, for scoring.
1. She wants to live in the United States
2. I want (to) _____.
3. I want to _____.
4. I want to go to _____.
5. I want to go at _____ P.M./A.M./o'clock.

Critical Thinking

Answers will vary. See Guidelines, page xx, for scoring.

Reading Answer Key

Answers 1, 3, and 4 are worth one point each; answer 2 is worth two points.
1. Travel Education Center   2. B.A. & Assoc.   3. 6/six   4. Academy of Art

Writing

Answers will vary. See Guidelines, page xviii, for scoring.

Worktext ✪✪✪

Listening Answer Key
1. b   2. b   3. b   4. c   5. a

Speaking

Either have students respond to you face to face, or have them record their responses on audiotapes. If administered face to face and learners have difficulty, do one of the following:

- move to the two-star assessment for Speaking.

- ask more detailed questions, such as the following:

  <u>for the meaning of the title</u>
  What people are in different worlds?
  How are the two worlds different?
  How does Miguel feel?
  How does Rosa feel?

  <u>for telling the story</u>
  Who comes to visit Rosa?
  What does Miguel give to Rosa?
  What does Miguel ask Rosa?
  What does she say?
  What does Miguel think of her plans for a restaurant?
  What does Rosa tell Miguel at the end?

Variation: Have learners respond to general statements such as the following.

  Tell about Miguel's visit.
  Tell about Rosa and Miguel.
  Tell what happens when Miguel asks Rosa to marry him.
  Tell what Rosa decides to do.

See Guidelines, page xv, for scoring.

Language Structure
See Guidelines, page xvi, for scoring.
1. Answer may vary. (I live in the United States because) I want to work.
2. Answer may vary. I want to get a better job.
3. Answer may vary. My family wants to buy a house.
4. What do you want?
5. What do you want to do?

Critical Thinking
Answers will vary. See Guidelines, page xx, for scoring.

Reading Answer Key
Each answer is worth two and one-half points.
Answers will vary. Possible answers:
1. Yes, because there are many kinds, such as waiter, cook, or manager; you can have a career
2. Yes, because people usually work during the day; it is convenient

Writing
Answers will vary. See Guidelines, page xix, for scoring.

Worlds Apart

Photo Stories

EXAMPLE	Miguel meets Jamal and Henry.

1. Rosa has a surprise for Miguel.
2. Rosa needs Henry's help.
3. Rosa has plans for a restaurant in Puebla.
4. Mr. Brashov gets a pillow from his brother.

Worktext All Levels

EXAMPLE	MRS. GILROY:	Well, how would you feel if you just lost your chef?
	MR. BRASHOV:	Ladies, I understand there is a problem with the chicken?
	MRS. GILROY:	It's not really a problem. It just tastes a little . . . different, that's all.
	OTHER WOMAN:	We're sorry to hear about your chef quitting.
	MR. BRASHOV:	Rosa, quitting?
	JESS:	I can explain that.
	MR. BRASHOV:	No, no, she is on her way back from the airport with Miguel.
	PEOPLE AT OTHER TABLES:	Oh.

1. ROSA: You want to sit down for awhile?
   CARRIE: I can't. You will never guess who I've got a date with tonight.
   ROSA: Not that cute guy from your office?
   CARRIE: That's right.
   ROSA: Hey, that's great, Carrie.
   CARRIE: Oh, by the way, you guys can have the place all to yourselves, if you want. I can stay with my friend, Heather.
   ROSA: No, that's okay. Miguel is staying at the Madison Hotel. Thanks anyway.
   CARRIE: Well, I'd better get ready.

2. MIGUEL: Rosa . . . will you marry me?

ROSA: I think I need to sit down.

MIGUEL: Are you really so surprised?

ROSA: I've thought about this day so many times. I just didn't think it would happen right now.

MIGUEL: I don't want us to be apart anymore.

ROSA: There are still so many things I want to do. I'm learning so much in my business classes and at the restaurant.

MIGUEL: But we don't have to get married right away. We could set the date for, perhaps, a year from now?

3. ROSA: You know, Miguel, I want to open my own restaurant. Maybe not now, but someday.

MIGUEL: That's wonderful.

ROSA: Yes, but I've always thought I'd do it in this country. Do you think it would be possible for you to move here, too?

MIGUEL: I would have to start my career all over again.

ROSA: But you can practice architecture anywhere, can't you?

MIGUEL: Rosita, Puebla is our home. It's where our families are. Our friends. Don't you ever get homesick?

ROSA: All the time. But I don't want to give up what I have here.

4. ROSA: That's the idea. If this is going to be like every other restaurant, why should we even bother?

MIGUEL: Maybe to have a successful business?

ROSA: Ah, you don't think my idea can be successful.

MIGUEL: Ay, mi amore. This is already different from what I was expecting. I must think about it.

ROSA: But I have <u>already</u> thought about it.

MIGUEL: Rosa, you are a very good chef. But there is more to opening a restaurant than just the cooking. There is the whole business side.

ROSA: That's why I'm taking classes at school.

MIGUEL: You can take as many classes as you want. But if you want to succeed in Puebla, you have to think like you live <u>there</u> . . . not <u>here</u>.

5. **MIGUEL:** Rosita . . . I don't want anything we said last night about the restaurant to change our plans.

   ROSA: Miguel, what happened last night wasn't about the restaurant. It was about us. It was about living in two very different worlds.

   MIGUEL: Only until you move back to Puebla.

   ROSA: Miguel, I love Mexico . . . I love my family. But I know if I go back to Pueblo as your wife, I would be going back to a life I left a long time ago.

Name   Date

Listening   Look at each picture. Listen to the tape. Write the letter of the correct picture on the line.

EXAMPLE   a.   b.

     _a_

1. _____   a.   b.

2. _____   a.   b.

3. _____   a.   b.

4. _____   a.   b.

Speaking   Jamal asks for help. How do his friends help? Think about your answer. Tell as much as you can. Your teacher will listen.

Reading   Look at each picture. Choose a, b, or c. Write the letter on the line.

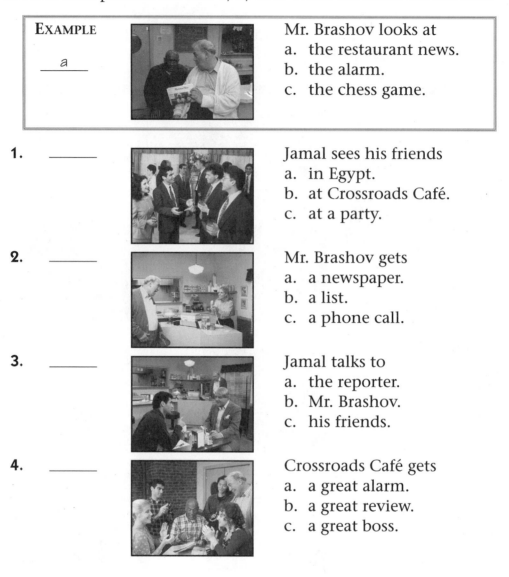

EXAMPLE   _a_   Mr. Brashov looks at
a. the restaurant news.
b. the alarm.
c. the chess game.

1. _____   Jamal sees his friends
a. in Egypt.
b. at Crossroads Café.
c. at a party.

2. _____   Mr. Brashov gets
a. a newspaper.
b. a list.
c. a phone call.

3. _____   Jamal talks to
a. the reporter.
b. Mr. Brashov.
c. his friends.

4. _____   Crossroads Café gets
a. a great alarm.
b. a great review.
c. a great boss.

Writing   Unscramble each word. Complete each sentence.

EXAMPLE   Jess reads the _n_ _e_ _w_ _s_ _p_ _a_ _p_ _e_ _r_
to the employees. (e s a e r p p w n)

1. The ___ ___ ___ ___ ___ ___ ___ writes for the newspaper.
(e r t p r o e r)

2. Jihan is ___ ___ ___ ___ ___ of her husband. (r o u p d)

3. Jamal can fix the ___ ___ ___ ___ ___. (l r m a a)

4. Jamal tells the ___ ___ ___ ___ ___ to his friends. (r t h u t)

Name _____   Date _____

Listening   Read each question. Watch the videotape. Circle the letter of the correct answer.

> EXAMPLE   How does Jess feel?
> (a.) ashamed
> b. weak
> c. angry

1. What are Jamal and Jihan talking about?
   a. Jamal's job at the restaurant
   b. Jamal's new business
   c. Jamal's lie about the restaurant

2. How does Katherine feel?
   a. happy
   b. angry
   c. disappointed

3. How does Mr. Brashov feel?
   a. confused
   b. sad
   c. happy

4. How does the reporter feel?
   a. happy
   b. confused
   c. disappointed

5. What does Jess have?
   a. a menu
   b. a title
   c. a restaurant review

Speaking   Talk about this picture. Tell as much as you can. Your teacher will listen.

Crossroads Café Assessment A   **4-3**

Language Structure   Make apologies.

EXAMPLE	You are Henry. You delivered the wrong order to a customer.
	I am sorry _that I delivered the wrong order._

1. You are Rosa. You forgot to cook a customer's order.

_____

2. You are Katherine. You didn't give a customer the correct change.

_____

3. You are Jamal. You couldn't fix the coffee maker.

_____

4. You are Jamal. You lied to your friend, Abdullah, about your job.

_____

5. You arrived late to class.

_____

Critical Thinking   Think about the question below. Write your ideas. Then talk about your ideas. Your teacher will listen.

Why did Jamal lie to his friends about his job?

_____

_____

_____

_____

_____

_____

_____

_____

_____   _____
Name   Date

Listening Read each question. Watch the videotape. Circle the letter of the correct answer.

EXAMPLE	What does Mr. Brashov think?
	(a.) Jess cannot hear.
	b. Jess has an arm problem.
	c. Jess is getting old.

1. What does Jihan tell Jamal?
   a. She is sorry for him.
   b. She is ashamed of him.
   c. She is proud of him.

2. What do Jamal's friends say about the restaurant?
   a. It's wonderful.
   b. It's pretentious.
   c. It's special.

3. What does Abdullah say?
   a. Jamal should get a new handyman.
   b. Jamal is a good handyman.
   c. Mr. Brashov is a good handyman.

4. What does Jamal think about fixing the alarm?
   a. He likes to do it.
   b. He wants to do it.
   c. He has to do it.

5. What does the article say about the food?
   a. It is tasty and beautiful.
   b. It is bad.
   c. It is occasionally good.

Speaking In this episode, Jamal let his friends from Egypt think that he was the owner of the café. Have you, or someone you know, ever had an experience when one lie grew into a big problem? Tell as much as you can. Your teacher will listen.

Language Structure   Make apologies.

EXAMPLE	You are late to work.
	I'm sorry <u>for being late.</u>
	OR
	I'm sorry <u>that I was late.</u>

1. You spilled coffee on a customer.

   _____

2. You forgot to give a friend a telephone message.

   _____

3. You broke a coworker's electric drill.

   _____

4. You are Jess. You argued with Mr. Brashov about your hearing problem.

   _____

5. You are Jamal. You lied to your friends about your job.

   _____

Critical Thinking   Think about the question below. Write your ideas. Then talk about your ideas. Your teacher will listen.

Would you lie to your friends about your job? Tell why or why not.

_____

_____

_____

_____

_____

_____

_____

4

_____   _____
Name   Date

Listening   Read each question. Watch the videotape. Circle the letter of the correct answer.

EXAMPLE	Why do Mr. Brashov and Jess arm wrestle?

> EXAMPLE   Why do Mr. Brashov and Jess arm wrestle?
> (a.) because Jess wants to prove he's strong
> b. because Mr. Brashov wants to prove he's strong
> c. because Mr. Brashov wants to prove Jess is not strong

1. What does Jamal think about his lie?
   a. It was harmful.
   b. It was important.
   c. It was unimportant.

2. Why does Jamal ask about Rosa's special?
   a. because he wants to check on Rosa's work
   b. because he wants to pretend to check on Rosa's work
   c. because he's really interested in it

3. Why does Katherine call Mr. Brashov "Victor?"
   a. to pretend she is the boss
   b. to pretend he is a worker like her
   c. to pretend he is the boss

4. What does the reporter say?
   a. He thought Mr. Brashov was the owner.
   b. He thought Jamal was the owner.
   c. He thought Katherine was the owner.

5. What did the reporter write about Mr. Brashov?
   a. He is a good businessman.
   b. He is a friendly businessman.
   c. He is both a good and a friendly businessman.

Speaking   Explain the title, "Who's the Boss?" or tell the story. Tell as much as you can. Your teacher will listen.

Crossroads Café Assessment A   **4-7**

Language Structure　　Make apologies.

EXAMPLE	You lied to your friend about your job.
	I'm sorry that I lied about my job.
	OR
	I'm sorry for lying about my job.

1. You broke some dishes.

   _____

2. You forgot a friend's birthday.

   _____

3. You lost your English book.

   _____

4. You missed an important meeting at work.

   _____

5. Make an apology for something you did recently.

   _____

Critical Thinking　　Think about the questions below. Write your ideas. Then talk about your ideas. Your teacher will listen.

Some people think they are their jobs. How about you? Are you your job? Tell why or why not.

_____

_____

_____

_____

_____

_____

_____

_____

Name   Date

Reading   Read the restaurant ad. Answer the questions.

> **The Old Main Inn**
> Restaurant and Bar
> 230 S. Front St., Winfield (630) 868-1660
>
> **SUNDAY BUFFET BRUNCH**
> Sunday Brunch served at 10 AM
> Adults **$7.95**   Kids under 10 **$4.95**
>
> *Featuring Sirloin Beef • Baked Ham • Baked Whitefish • Pepper Steak*
> *• BBQ Ribs • Spinach Pie • Baked Mostaccioli • Salad Bar • Fresh Fruits*
> *• French Toast • Pancakes • Eggs • Sausage • Juice • Coffee*
>
> **SUNDAY SPECIALS**
> Roast Loin of Pork with homemade dressing 6.95
> Roast Sirloin of Beef Au Jus 7.95
> Roast Turkey with dressing 6.95
> Grecian Style Chicken 5.95
>
> All above served with Bowl of Soup or Salad, Choice of Potato, Rolls, and Butter
> All Major Credit Cards Accepted
>
> Open 7 Days: Sun. - Thurs. 11 AM - 1 AM; Fri. - Sat. 11 AM - 2 AM

✪ **1.** What time is Sunday Brunch served? _____

2. How many days a week is the restaurant open? _____

3. What time does the restaurant open on Friday? _____

4. What time does the restaurant close on Thursday? _____

5. How much does the Sunday Brunch cost for adults? _____

✪✪ **1.** Is the restaurant open on Sunday nights?   YES   NO
2. Is coffee included with the Sunday Brunch?   YES   NO
3. Do the Sunday Specials include soup or salad?   YES   NO
4. Is Sunday Brunch free for children under 5?   YES   NO
5. Can you have fresh fruit with the Sunday Brunch?   YES   NO

✪✪✪ **1.** Is the restaurant open for lunch on weekdays?   YES   NO
2. Can children eat at this restaurant?   YES   NO
3. If you don't eat meat, can you have the Sunday Brunch? YES   NO
4. Can you use a credit card to pay for your meal?   YES   NO
5. If you have a small appetite, should you order the Sunday Brunch? Tell why or why not.

_____

_____

Writing   In this unit, you wrote a review of a restaurant. Now write a review for The Old Main Inn.

Crossroads Café Assessment A   **4-9**

Learner Checklist

1. Rate yourself.

I CAN . . .	ALWAYS	SOMETIMES	NEVER
make apologies.	❏	❏	❏
read a newspaper ad.	❏	❏	❏
write a restaurant review.	❏	❏	❏
talk about strategies for making a job change.	❏	❏	❏

2. Meet with your teacher. Talk about how successful you were in reaching the goals for this unit. Compare how you rated yourself with how your teacher rated you.

3. Think about your rating and your teacher's rating. What do you need to study more?

_____

_____

_____

fold --- fold

Instructor Checklist

1. Rate the learner. For each item, circle a number based on the following scale.

   3 = easily understood, 2 = understood with difficulty, 1 = not understood

THE LEARNER CAN . . .	RATING	COMMENTS
make apologies.	1 2 3	
read a newspaper ad.	1 2 3	
write a restaurant review.	1 2 3	
talk about strategies for making a job change.	1 2 3	

2. Meet with the learner. Use the two completed checklists to talk about learner outcomes in this unit and priorities for further study.

Photo Stories

— Listening Answer Key
1. b   **2.** b   **3.** a   **4.** a

— Speaking
Either have students respond to you face to face, or have students record their responses on audiotapes. See Guidelines, page xii, for scoring.

— Reading Answer Key
1. c   **2.** c   **3.** a   **4.** b

— Writing Answer Key
1. reporter   **2.** proud   **3.** alarm   **4.** truth

Worktext ✪

— Listening Answer Key
1. c   **2.** b   **3.** a   **4.** b   **5.** c

— Speaking
Either have students respond to you face to face, or have students record their responses on audiotapes. See Guidelines, page xiii, for scoring.

— Language Structure
See Guidelines, page xvi, for scoring.

— Critical Thinking
Answers will vary. See Guidelines, page xx, for scoring.

— Reading Answer Key
Each answer is worth one point.
1. at 10:00 A.M.   **2.** 7 days   **3.** at 11:00 A.M.   **4.** at 1:00 A.M.   **5.** $7.95

— Writing Answer Key
Answers will vary. See Guidelines, page xvii, for scoring.

Worktext ✪✪

— Listening Answer Key
1. c   **2.** a   **3.** a   **4.** c   **5.** a

— Speaking
Either have students respond to you face to face, or have students record their responses on audiotapes. If learners are unable to respond, do one of the following:

• move to the one-star assessment for Speaking.

- ask more detailed questions about the episode.

Variation: Ask questions about pictures in Before You Watch, page 44.
See Guidelines, page xiv, for scoring.

Language Structure
See Guidelines, page xvi, for scoring.

Critical Thinking
Answers will vary. See Guidelines, page xx, for scoring.

Reading Answer Key
Each answer is worth one point.
1. yes   **2.** yes   **3.** yes   **4.** no   **5.** yes

Writing
Answers will vary. See Guidelines, page xviii, for scoring.

Worktext ✪✪✪

Listening Answer Key
1. c   **2.** b   **3.** b   **4.** a   **5.** c

Speaking
Either have students respond to you face to face, or have them record their responses on audiotapes. If administered face-to-face and learners have difficulty,

- move to the two-star assessment for Speaking.
- ask more detailed questions, such as:

  <u>for the meaning of the title</u>
  Who lied about his job?
  Who lied to pretend Jamal was the boss?
  Who was confused by all the lies?

  <u>for telling the story</u>
  Why did Jamal lie about his job?
  Why did the reporter come to the restaurant?
  Why was Jess confused?
  What does Jamal learn about telling the truth?
  What does the reporter learn about Mr. Brashov?

Variation: Have learners respond to general statements such as:
Tell about the burglar alarm.
Tell about the party.
Tell about the restaurant review and how you think everyone feels about it.
Tell what you think everyone believes about Mr. Brashov.

See Guidelines, page xv, for scoring.

— **Language Structure**
See Guidelines, page xvi, for scoring.

— **Critical Thinking**
Answers will vary. See Guidelines, page xx, for scoring.

— **Reading Answer Key**
Each answer is worth one point.
1. yes　　**2.** yes　　**3.** yes　　**4.** yes　　**5.** No. Reasons will vary.

— **Writing Answer Key**
See Guidelines, page xix, for scoring.

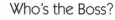

Photo Stories

EXAMPLE	Mr. Brashov looks at the *Restaurant News*.

1. Jamal and Jihan like the party.
2. Jamal's friends come to the restaurant.
3. Jamal talks to the reporter.
4. Jamal is ashamed.

Worktext All Levels

EXAMPLE	MR. BRASHOV:	Jess, my friend. I think you may be having a hearing problem.
	JESS:	Are you kidding me? My hearing is just as good as it ever was.
	MR. BRASHOV:	I'm sorry, Jess, I don't think it is. But that's nothing to be ashamed of.
	JESS:	I may be getting old, but I'm just as fit as a young man. You don't believe me? Come on, I'll prove it to you!
	MR. BRASHOV:	What are you doing?
	JESS:	I'm challenging you to an arm wrestle.
	MR. BRASHOV:	Come on, this is silly.
	JESS:	I'll show you who's old and weak.

1. JIHAN: Oh, Gamal. Why didn't you say something?

   JAMAL: I'm sorry but I couldn't just tell them the truth. When they knew me, I was an important civil engineer. And now I am just a handyman.

   JIHAN: You should not be ashamed of what you do. You work very hard. I am proud of you.

   JAMAL: So it was only a small lie. What harm could it possibly do? Hmm!

2. **JAMAL:**   Katherine, bring over some coffee. And ah . . . where is Henry? He should be back from the delivery by now. . . . So, my friends, how do you like my restaurant?

   ABDULLAH: It's a wonderful little place

   MOHAMMED: Very charming.

   JAMAL: It is, isn't it. Nothing pretentious. Rosa, how are you doing on tomorrow's special?

   ROSA: Excuse me???

   KATHERINE: What do you think you are doing?

   JAMAL: Come along now, Katherine. You have work to do. Excuse us one moment.

   KATHERINE: You can't tell me what to do.

   ROSA: Are you feeling O.K.?

3. **MR. BRASHOV:** Jamal, all the wires are connected. Does that mean the burglar alarm is working?

   JAMAL: I don't know. You tell me.

   MR. BRASHOV: What do you mean, tell me? Who is the handyman around here?

   JAMAL: Um . . . you are?

   MR. BRASHOV: I am?

   KATHERINE: Oh, Victor, may I talk to you for a moment, please?

   MR. BRASHOV: "Victor?" What is going on here?

   ABDULLAH: That handyman seems to have a bad attitude, if you don't mind me saying so, perhaps you should replace him.

4. **JAMAL:**   I'd better do it.

   ABDULLAH: But Jamal, isn't that the handyman's job?

   JAMAL: Yes. It is the handyman's job. And I am the handyman.

   REPORTER: Then, if I'm not mistaken, that makes you the owner of this restaurant?

   JAMAL: Yes, this is the owner, Mr. Victor Brashov.

   REPORTER: I had a hunch that was the case.

5. JESS: The title is—"Crossroads Café—Who's the Boss?" "Not only does Victor Brashov run a successful restaurant, but he is a good friend to his employees. On one occasion, he even let one of them pose as the owner. . . ."

MR. BRASHOV: Does it mention about how delicious the food is?

JESS: He mentions that, too.

ROSA: What about how beautifully the meals are presented?

JESS: He says that next.

Name _____ Date _____

Listening Look at each picture. Listen to the tape. Write the letter of the correct picture on the line.

> **EXAMPLE** a. b.
>
> ___b___

1. _____ a. b.

2. _____ a. b.

3. _____ a. b.

4. _____ a. b.

Speaking What does David learn from Jess? Think about your answer. Tell as much as you can. Your teacher will listen.

 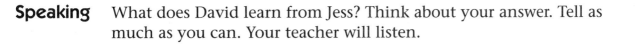

Reading   Look at each picture. Choose a, b, or c. Write the letter on the line.

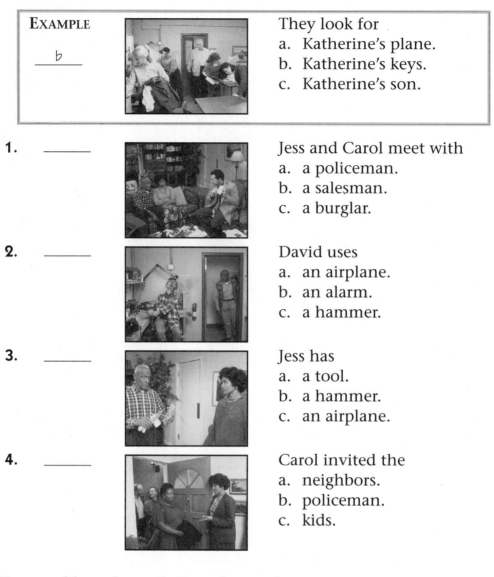

EXAMPLE

___b___

They look for
a. Katherine's plane.
b. Katherine's keys.
c. Katherine's son.

1. _____

Jess and Carol meet with
a. a policeman.
b. a salesman.
c. a burglar.

2. _____

David uses
a. an airplane.
b. an alarm.
c. a hammer.

3. _____

Jess has
a. a tool.
b. a hammer.
c. an airplane.

4. _____

Carol invited the
a. neighbors.
b. policeman.
c. kids.

Writing   Unscramble each word. Complete each sentence.

EXAMPLE   They look for Katherine's __k__ __e__ __y__ __s__ . (e y s k)

1. David can see a ___ ___ ___ ___ ___ ___ ___ ___ ___ at school.
   (o n e o r l s u c)

2. Jamal uses ___ ___ ___ ___ ___ to install the alarm. (t o s l o)

3. Carol doesn't want any steel ___ ___ ___ ___ on her house. (a s r b)

4. Carol invites ___ ___ ___ ___ ___ ___ ___ ___ . They live
   near her house. (s n e r i o g b h)

5

Lost and Found

Name _____   Date _____

Listening Read each question. Watch the videotape. Circle the letter of the correct answer.

> EXAMPLE   What is the policeman reporting?
> a. a car accident
> (b.) a burglary
> c. a fight

1. What are Jess and Carol arguing about?
   a. money
   b. security
   c. work

2. How does Katherine feel about her son?
   a. proud
   b. amused
   c. frustrated

3. What is the man selling?
   a. windows
   b. telephones
   c. alarms

4. What are Jess and David talking about?
   a. airplanes
   b. fathers
   c. friends

5. What are Jess and Carol talking about?
   a. Carol's friends
   b. Carol's job
   c. Carol's safety

Speaking Talk about this picture. Tell as much as you can. Your teacher will listen.

Language Structure

Tell someone to do something.

EXAMPLE	You will break the window if you play in here.
	Give me _the ball._____

1. You can not play ball inside the restaurant.

   Get _____

2. May I look at that alarm, please?

   Sure, take _____

3. How do I set the alarm?

   Punch in _____

4. The alarm is very loud.

   Please cover _____

5. How do I fix the alarm?

   Place the green wire beneath the blue _____

Critical Thinking

Think about the question below. Write your ideas. Then talk about your ideas. Your teacher will listen.

Do you think Jess and his wife, Carol, can keep their home safe? Tell why or why not.

_____

_____

_____

_____

_____

_____

_____

_____

_____

_____

Name   Date

Listening   Read each question. Watch the videotape. Circle the letter of the correct answer.

> **EXAMPLE**   What was taken from Carol and Jess' house?
> a. money
> (b.) appliances
> c. jewelry

1. What does Jess want?
   a. to get locks and alarms
   b. to punish the burglars
   c. to move to a new house

2. What are Katherine and David arguing about?
   a. David's friends
   b. David's watch
   c. David's schoolwork

3. What is the "A" package?
   a. the cheapest security system
   b. the most expensive security system
   c. a mid-priced security system

4. What does Jess say about his father?
   a. He left home.
   b. He lost his job.
   c. He was a pilot.

5. What does Jess want Carol to do?
   a. wake up earlier
   b. come home earlier
   c. make dinner earlier

Speaking   In this episode, Katherine has problems with her son. What advice do you have for parents like Katherine? What should they do to help their children? Tell as much as you can. Your teacher will listen.

Language Structure   Tell someone to do something.

EXAMPLE	What should I do after school?
	Come home.

1. What should I do about this messy room?

   _____

2. How can I help you with dinner?

   _____

3. What would you like me to do after dinner?

   _____

4. Who should I talk to about this difficult homework?

   _____

5. What can I do to improve my English?

   _____

Critical Thinking   Think about the question below. Write your ideas. Then talk about your ideas. Your teacher will listen.

Do you think neighbors can work together to protect their neighborhoods? Tell why or why not.

   _____

   _____

   _____

   _____

   _____

   _____

   _____

   _____

   _____

_____   _____
Name   Date

Listening   Read each question. Watch the videotape. Circle the letter of the
              correct answer.

EXAMPLE	What happened during the burglary?

EXAMPLE   What happened during the burglary?
              (a.) No one was home, and some things were stolen.
              b. Carol was home, and some things were stolen.
              c. Carol and Jess were both home, and nothing was stolen.

1. How does Carol feel?
    a. She wants more security in the house.
    b. She doesn't want too much security in the house.
    c. She wants less security in the house.

2. Why is Katherine so upset?
    a. David lied about the watch.
    b. David broke the watch.
    c. David lost the watch.

3. How do Jess and Carol feel about getting a home security
    system?
    a. They are not interested in home security.
    b. They are worried about the price of home security.
    c. They will pay any price to have home security.

4. How do Jess and David feel about their fathers?
    a. They are both angry at their fathers for leaving.
    b. David is angry at his father for leaving, but Jess isn't.
    c. David isn't angry at his father for leaving, but Jess is.

5. What are Jess and Carol arguing about?
    a. Jess wants to stay out late with his friends.
    b. Jess wants Carol to come home early.
    c. Carol wants Jess to go out with her more.

Speaking   Explain the title, "Lost and Found," or tell the story. Tell as much
              as you can. Your teacher will listen.

Language Structure   Tell someone to do something.

EXAMPLE	Is the bus coming now?
	Yes, hurry up.

1. How can I carry all of these books?

   _____

2. Is there anything we can do about the loud music?

   _____

3. How do I set the watch?

   _____

4. What should we do about crime prevention?

   _____

5. How can I improve my English?

   _____

Critical Thinking   Think about the question below. Write your ideas. Then talk about your ideas. Your teacher will listen.

Do you think there is a lot of crime in the United States? Tell why or why not.

_____

_____

_____

_____

_____

_____

_____

_____

_____

_____

Name _____   Date _____

Reading   Read the pamphlet on Fire Prevention. Answer the questions.

FIRE PREVENTION INSIDE THE HOME	Flammable Liquids	non-emergency telephone number for more information.

FIRE PREVENTION INSIDE THE HOME

Smoking
• Do not smoke in bed. Throw all cigarette butts and used matches in the toilet.

Kitchen
• Do not leave the kitchen when cooking. Keep towels and paper away from the stove. Be able to identify the smell of natural gas from a gas stove. Call the gas company right away if you smell it.

Heating
• Have a qualified person clean your furnace regularly. Keep small heating units away from drapes, carpets, and clothing.

Flammable Liquids
• Do not use near fire or flame. Do not put on stove, radiator, or other place where the temperature will be higher than 120° F. Read the directions on the container.

OUTSIDE THE HOME

Garbage
• Do not leave wood, paper, and other flammable material outside. Store properly or put in the garbage can. Cover the garbage can.

Disposing of Fuels
• Federal and state EPA (Environmental Protection Agency) laws exist about throwing away motor oil, gasoline, etc. Call your local fire department's

non-emergency telephone number for more information.

GENERAL INFORMATION

Electrical Safety
• Check your appliances for UL safety seals. This means they have been tested for safety. Find and check all electrical cords. They should not be old. Call the electric company if you have questions.

Smoke/Fire Detector
• Buy good smoke/fire detectors. Install them in your home and garage according to directions.

Plan
• Keep the telephone number of the fire department near all telephones. Talk to your family about escape routes.

✪ 1. Fire prevention is important inside and outside the house.   YES   NO

2. Electrical safety is important in fire prevention.   YES   NO

3. The pamphlet advises you to smoke in bed.   YES   NO

4. You need to buy good smoke/fire detectors.   YES   NO

5. Leave the kitchen when you cook.   YES   NO

✪✪ 1. Keep a small heating unit near your clothes to warm them.   YES   NO

2. The UL safety seal on an appliance means the appliance has been tested for safety.   YES   NO

3. You can throw away motor oil wherever you want.   YES   NO

4. Plan to keep the telephone number of the fire department near the telephone.   YES   NO

5. Garbage should be covered.   YES   NO

✪✪✪ 1. The federal law about fuels means the United States wants to protect people and the environment.   YES   NO

2. The pamphlet discourages calls to the fire department or electric company for more information.   YES   NO

3. You can do many things to prevent a fire.   YES   NO

4. An escape route is a useless idea for your safety from fire.   YES   NO

5. Smoke detectors are safety devices for fire prevention.   YES   NO

Writing   In this episode, a burglar broke in to Jess's house. Write a letter to Jess's son. Tell him the things to do to prevent a burglary.

Learner Checklist

1. Rate yourself.

I CAN . . .	ALWAYS	SOMETIMES	NEVER
tell someone to do something.	❏	❏	❏
read about home security.	❏	❏	❏
write a letter describing a burglary.	❏	❏	❏
talk about ways to prevent neighborhood crime.	❏	❏	❏

2. Meet with your teacher. Talk about how successful you were in reaching the goals for this unit. Compare how you rated yourself with how your teacher rated you.

3. Think about your rating and your teacher's rating. What do you need to study more?

_____

_____

_____

fold --- fold

Instructor Checklist

1. Rate the learner. For each item, circle a number based on the following scale.

   3 = easily understood, 2 = understood with difficulty, 1 = not understood

THE LEARNER CAN . . .	RATING	COMMENTS
tell someone to do something.	1 2 3	
read about home security.	1 2 3	
write a letter describing a burglary.	1 2 3	
talk about ways to prevent neighborhood crime.	1 2 3	

2. Meet with the learner. Use the two completed checklists to talk about learner outcomes in this unit and priorities for further study.

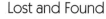
Photo Stories

— Listening Answer Key
1. a   **2.** b   **3.** a   **4.** b

— Speaking
Either have students respond to you face to face, or have students record their responses on audiotapes. See Guidelines, page xii, for scoring.

— Reading Answer Key
1. b   **2.** c   **3.** c   **4.** a

— Writing Answer Key
1. counselor   **2.** tools   **3.** bars   **4.** neighbors

Worktext ✪

— Listening Answer Key
1. b   **2.** c   **3.** c   **4.** b   **5.** c

— Speaking
Either have students respond to you face to face, or have students record their responses on audiotapes. See Guidelines, page xiii, for scoring.

— Language Structure
See Guidelines, page xvi, for scoring.
1. out (of here).   **2.** a look.   **3.** the code/numbers/buttons.   **4.** your ears.
5. wire.

— Critical Thinking
Answers will vary. See Guidelines, page xx, for scoring.

— Reading Answer Key
Each answer is worth one point.
1. yes   **2.** yes   **3.** no   **4.** yes   **5.** no

— Writing
Answers will vary. See Guidelines, page xvii, for scoring.

Worktext ✪✪

— Listening Answer Key
1. a   **2.** b   **3.** b   **4.** a   **5.** b

— Speaking

Either have students respond to you face to face, or have them record their responses on audiotapes. If administered face to face and learners are unable to respond, do one of the following:

- move to the one-star assessment for Speaking.
- ask more specific questions about the episode, such as

  "Tell me what happened when David and his friends came into the restaurant."
  OR
  "What happened to Jess and Carol? What did they do about it?"

Variation: Ask questions about pictures in Before You Watch (p. 58). For example, point to picture #2 and ask: "What are Jess and Carol doing?" "What are they saying?" "How do they feel?"

See Guidelines, page xiv, for scoring.

— Language Structure

Answers will vary. See Guidelines, page xvi, for scoring.

1. Clean it up.
2. Set the table./Cook the rice.
3. Do the dishes./Do your homework.
4. Call your friend./Ask your teacher.
5. Study harder./Take classes./Do your homework.

— Critical Thinking

Answers will vary. See Guidelines, page xx, for scoring.

— Reading Answer Key

Each answer is worth one point.

1. no   2. yes   3. no   4. yes   5. yes

— Writing

Answers will vary. See Guidelines, page xviii, for scoring.

Worktext ✪✪✪

— Listening Answer Key

1. b   2. a   3. b   4. a   5. b

— Speaking

Either have students respond to you face to face, have them record their responses on audiotapes. If administered face to face and learners are unable to respond, do one of the following:

- move to the two-star assessment for Speaking.

- ask more detailed questions, such as:

  <u>for the meaning of the title</u>

  Who was lost, and who "found" each other again?
  Why was David in trouble?
  How did Katherine feel about her son?
  What did Jess and David talk about?
  How did David feel after talking to Jess?

  <u>for telling the story</u>

  What happened to Jess and Carol?
  What does Jess want to do about it?
  How does Carol feel?
  What do they do to solve the problem?
  What did David do that upset his mother?
  How does Jess help David?

Variation: Have learners respond to general statements such as the following.

Tell about the problems in Katherine's family.
Tell how the problems in the family are resolved.
Tell about the break-in at Jess and Carol's house.
Tell what they did about the break-in at their house.

See Guidelines, page xv, for scoring.

Language Structure

Answers will vary. See Guidelines, page xvi, for scoring.

1. Give them/some to me/Put them down.
2. Turn it down./Cover your ears.
3. Push the button on the right./Punch in the code.
4. Talk to police or neighbors./Call the police./Get an alarm./Lock the doors.
5. Do your homework./Study hard./Speak./Practice with your teacher.

Critical Thinking

Answers will vary. See Guidelines, page xx, for scoring.

Reading Answer Key

Each answer is worth one point.

1. yes   2. no   3. yes   4. no   5. yes

Writing

Answers will vary. See Guidelines, page xix, for scoring.

Photo Stories

EXAMPLE	They look for Katherine's keys.

1. Mr. Brashov tells the boys to leave.
2. Jess sees David in the utility room.
3. Jamal tries to install the alarm.
4. Katherine gets a phone call about her son.

Worktext All Levels

EXAMPLE	**POLICE:**	Do you have a list of what's missing?
	CAROL:	No, not yet. I know they got the VCR and an old TV.
	JESS:	What else did they get?
	CAROL:	The toaster oven.
	JESS:	The toaster oven?
	POLICE:	Yup. You'd be surprised what people will take.
	JESS:	I can't believe they did this in broad daylight. What would they have done if you'd been here when they broke in?

1. **JESS:** First thing tomorrow, I'm going to make some calls . . . maybe get some security companies to come out here.

   CAROL: Jess, let's not overreact. Nobody was hurt. We're both fine.

   JESS: This time. But what about next time and the time after that?

   CAROL: All I know is, I've seen Mrs. Wilson's house with the bars and the steel doors . . . and I'm not going to live like that.

   JESS: Well, I'm not going to live like this.

2. **KATHERINE:** Where'd you get the watch?

   DAVID: I found it at school.

   KATHERINE: When?

   DAVID: I don't know. What's the big deal? Maybe a few days ago.

   KATHERINE: That's pretty unlikely, since you haven't been in school all week.

   DAVID: Who says?

   KATHERINE: Your school counselor.

3. JESS: What about the alarms?

KINKAID: Oh, we've got that. We've got it all. Infrared sensors. Motion detectors. Closed circuit cameras. Twenty-four-hour-a-day monitoring. Plus, we can provide you with portable devices that will disable any attacker . . . all fully legal, of course.

CAROL: Of course.

JESS: What's all this going to cost?

KINKAID: I'm glad you asked that. We've got a special going on this month, a red tag special, on our "A" package.

CAROL: Your "A" package?

KINKAID: That's our top-of-the-line, deluxe system. You go with that, I guarantee you, nobody's going to get near you.

4. DAVID: I used to build stuff with my dad.

JESS: What do you mean used to?

DAVID: My parents are divorced.

JESS: Ah. You see him much?

DAVID: We got a call last Christmas. No big deal.

JESS: Yeah. That's what I used to say. My dad left when I was ten. Never really found out why. I woke up one morning and there was a note on the table . . . and next to it was an old-fashioned airplane carved out of wood.

DAVID: An airplane?

JESS: Yeah. My dad made it himself. Real nice job. I guess he thought it would make me feel less angry. It didn't.

5. CAROL: Hi, Jess.

JESS: Where have you been, Carol? I have been worried about you.

CAROL: Jess, it's only eight-thirty . . . and last time I looked I was well over 21.

JESS: I just don't think it's safe for you to go places alone, especially at night. I'm thinking if you're in by seven-thirty, eight at the latest, you've got a better chance.

CAROL: You're giving me a curfew?

JESS: Not a curfew. Just a reminder that it's safer to be home behind locked doors.

CAROL: I don't believe this. Next thing you'll be telling me to call you when I get to the supermarket. Jess, I'm not a child.

JESS: Carol, I'm just trying to do what's right.

6

Name _____   Date _____

Listening   Look at each picture. Listen to the tape. Write the letter of the correct picture on the line.

EXAMPLE	a.	b.
_a_		

1. _____   a.   b.

2. _____   a.   b.

3. _____   a.   b.

4. _____   a.   b.

Speaking   How does Emery change the café? Think about the answer. Tell as much as you can. Your teacher will listen.

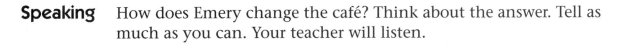

Reading   Look at each picture. Choose a, b, or c. Write the letter on the line.

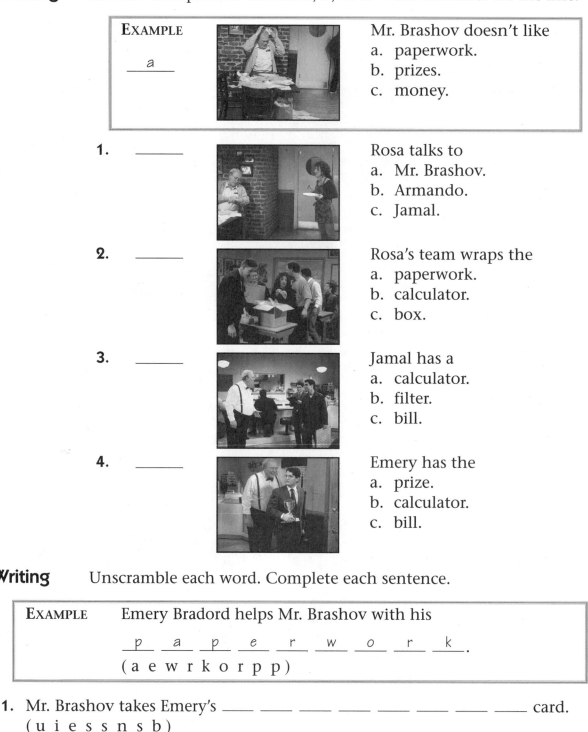

EXAMPLE

_a_

Mr. Brashov doesn't like
a. paperwork.
b. prizes.
c. money.

1. _____

Rosa talks to
a. Mr. Brashov.
b. Armando.
c. Jamal.

2. _____

Rosa's team wraps the
a. paperwork.
b. calculator.
c. box.

3. _____

Jamal has a
a. calculator.
b. filter.
c. bill.

4. _____

Emery has the
a. prize.
b. calculator.
c. bill.

Writing   Unscramble each word. Complete each sentence.

EXAMPLE   Emery Bradord helps Mr. Brashov with his

   _p_ _a_ _p_ _e_ _r_ _w_ _o_ _r_ _k_ .
(a e w r k o r p p)

1. Mr. Brashov takes Emery's ___ ___ ___ ___ ___ ___ ___ card.
(u i e s s n s b)

2. Mr. Brashov is more ___ ___ ___ ___ ___ ___ ___ ___ ___.
(o g n z d e i a r)

3. Rosa wins the ___ ___ ___ ___ ___ ___. (o t t s e n c)

4. Emery wants the workers to be ___ ___ ___ ___ ___ ___ ___ ___ ___.
(f i i t e n c f e)

Name _____ Date _____

Listening Read each question. Watch the videotape. Circle the letter of the correct answer.

EXAMPLE   Who is Katherine waiting for?
     a. Mr. Brashov
     (b.) Henry
     c. her children

1. What is Jess looking for?
   a. a business card
   b. a paper
   c. a lucky number

2. How much is the prize?
   a. $1,000
   b. $100
   c. $10

3. What are Jamal, Emery, and Mr. Brashov talking about?
   a. saving money
   b. using the telephone book
   c. saving time

4. How does Rosa feel?
   a. happy
   b. worried
   c. angry

5. How does Emery feel?
   a. happy
   b. excited
   c. confused

Speaking Talk about this picture. Tell as much as you can. Your teacher will listen.

Language Structure   Make suggestions.

EXAMPLE	I don't like my job.
	Why don't you <u>look for another job?</u>

1. My car is 12 years old, and it needs a lot of repairs.

   Why don't you _____

2. This English class is too easy for me.

   Why don't you _____

3. I forget my dentist appointments.

   Why don't you _____

4. I don't have time to eat breakfast.

   Why don't you _____

5. I have a sore throat and a headache.

   Why don't you _____

Critical Thinking   Think about the question below. Write your ideas. Then talk about your ideas. Your teacher will listen.

Do you think it is important to save time or money? Tell why or why not.

_____

_____

_____

_____

_____

_____

_____

_____

_____

_____

6

_____

Name

Date

Listening   Read each question. Watch the videotape. Circle the letter of the correct answer.

> **EXAMPLE**   What is Katherine talking about?
> a. Mr. Brashov is late again.
> b. Henry is late again.
> c. Her children are late again.

1. What does Jess want Mr. Brashov to do?
   a. help his son
   b. meet his son's friend
   c. take his son's business card

2. Why does Emery think the employees can continue to work so fast?
   a. because they like to run around
   b. because they want to win the contest
   c. because they are investing in the future

3. What does Emery tell Mr. Brashov?
   a. Saving money at work is very important.
   b. Friendship at work is very important.
   c. Joe's Hardware is very important.

4. What does Rosa's teacher say?
   a. A good manager runs a good team.
   b. A good manager runs a good business.
   c. A good manager is part of the team.

5. What does Mr. Brashov tell Emery?
   a. He has done enough at the restaurant.
   b. He will continue to work at the restaurant.
   c. He has won $100.

Speaking   In this episode, Mr. Brashov had problems getting organized. Emery came to help him save time and money. Think about your experiences at work or at home. Is it always important to save money or time? Tell why or why not. Tell as much as you can. Your teacher will listen.

Language Structure Make suggestions.

EXAMPLE	I can't go to English class this week.
	Why don't you ask your teacher for extra homework?
	OR
	Maybe you should ask your teacher for extra homework.
	OR
	How about asking your teacher for extra homework?

1. I don't understand the meaning of this word.

   _____

2. The remote control for the television doesn't work.

   _____

3. This milk smells sour.

   _____

4. I'm not interested in this television program.

   _____

5. I need some exercise.

   _____

Critical Thinking Think about the question below. Write your ideas. Then talk about your ideas. Your teacher will listen.

Do you agree that making money is the most important thing in business? Tell why or why not.

_____

_____

_____

_____

_____

_____

Name   Date

Listening   Read each question. Watch the videotape. Circle the letter of the correct answer.

> **EXAMPLE**   What does Katherine want Mr. Brashov to do?
> a. help her with the dishes
> b. pick up her kids
> c. talk to Henry

1. What does Mr. Brashov think about Jess's suggestion?
   a. He likes it a lot.
   b. He likes it a little.
   c. He doesn't like it.

2. What does Mr. Brashov really think about the contest?
   a. He is happy his employees are working so fast.
   b. He is making a good investment.
   c. He is not sure his employees can continue to work so fast.

3. Why does Jamal go to Bidwell's?
   a. He is following Emery's advice.
   b. He is following Mr. Brashov's advice.
   c. He is following Joe's advice.

4. Why is Rosa unhappy?
   a. The teacher thinks she won't be a good manager.
   b. The other students think she won't be a good manager.
   c. She thinks she won't be a good manager.

5. What is Mr. Brashov's advice to Emery?
   a. He should use his skills to continue to help Crossroads Café.
   b. He should use his skills to start his own business.
   c. He should use his skills to help another business.

Speaking   Explain the title, "Time is Money," or tell the story. Tell as much as you can. Your teacher will listen.

Language Structure   Make suggestions.

EXAMPLE	I didn't understand this newspaper story.
	Why don't you read it again?
	OR
	Maybe you should read it again.
	OR
	How about reading it again?

1. My new VCR doesn't work.

   _____

2. The new English teacher speaks too quickly.

   _____

3. I can't find my house keys.

   _____

4. I don't have time to do my English homework.

   _____

5. I think my paycheck has an error.

   _____

Critical Thinking   Think about the sentence below. Write your ideas. Then talk about your ideas. Your teacher will listen.

Do you agree that time is money? Tell why or why not.

_____

_____

_____

_____

_____

_____

_____

6

Name _____   Date _____

Reading   Read the Community Recreation Department schedule. Answer the questions.

WINTER/SPRING ACTIVITY GUIDE		
Ballroom Dancing	F	8:00–10:00 P.M.
Cake Decorating	TH	7:30–9:30 P.M
Dog Obedience Training	F	7:30–9:00 P.M
Get Fit Fast Exercise Class	M-W-F	6:30–7:30 P.M
Keyboarding—Beginning	M	7:00–9:00 P.M
Keyboarding—Intermediate	W	7:00–9:00 P.M
Volleyball	T-TH	8:00–10:00 P.M

✪ **1.** What day is Ballroom Dancing? _____

2. What time does it begin? _____

3. What day is Intermediate Keyboarding? _____

4. What time does it end? _____

5. What day is Cake Decorating? _____

✪✪ **1.** How long is the Cake Decorating class? _____

2. How long is the Dog Obedience Training class? _____

3. How many Keyboarding classes are there? _____

4. How many hours a week can you play volleyball? _____

5. How many days a week can you go to exercise class? _____

✪✪✪ **1.** Can you take both Ballroom Dancing and Dog Obedience Training? Tell why or why not. _____

_____

2. If you take Get Fit Fast, can you take any other classes? Tell why or why not. _____

_____

Writing   Write a letter to a friend. Tell about Emery, his suggestions, and how others felt about his suggestions.

Crossroads Café Assessment A   **6-9**

Learner Checklist

1. Rate yourself.

I CAN . . .	ALWAYS	SOMETIMES	NEVER
make suggestions.	❑	❑	❑
read schedules.	❑	❑	❑
write a letter.	❑	❑	❑
talk about U.S. attitudes about time.	❑	❑	❑

2. Meet with your teacher. Talk about how successful you were in reaching the goals for this unit. Compare how you rated yourself with how your teacher rated you.

3. Think about your rating and your teacher's rating. What do you need to study more?

_____

_____

_____

fold -- **fold**

Instructor Checklist

1. Rate the learner. For each item, circle a number based on the following scale.

3 = easily understood, 2 = understood with difficulty, 1 = not understood

THE LEARNER CAN . . .	RATING	COMMENTS
make suggestions.	1 2 3	
read schedules.	1 2 3	
write a letter.	1 2 3	
talk about U.S. attitudes about time.	1 2 3	

2. Meet with the learner. Use the two completed checklists to talk about learner outcomes in this unit and priorities for further study.

Photo Stories

— Listening Answer Key
1. a   **2.** b   **3.** a   **4.** a

— Speaking
Either have students respond to you face to face, or have students record their responses on audiotapes. See Guidelines, page xii, for scoring.

— Reading Answer Key
1. a   **2.** c   **3.** b   **4.** a

— Writing Answer Key
1. business   **2.** organized   **3.** contest   **4.** efficient

Worktext ✪

— Listening Answer Key
1. a   **2.** b   **3.** a   **4.** b   **5.** c

— Speaking
Either have students respond to you face to face, or have students record their responses on audiotapes. See Guidelines, page xiii, for scoring.

— Language Structure
Answers may vary; possible answers are provided. See Guidelines, page xvi, for scoring.
1. Why don't you buy a new car?
2. Why don't you take a different class? OR Why don't you take a more advanced class?
3. Why don't you call the dentist? OR Why don't you write the appointments on a calendar?
4. Why don't you get up earlier?
5. Why don't you call the doctor? OR Why don't you take some medicine?

— Critical Thinking
Answers will vary. See Guidelines, page xx, for scoring.

— Reading Answer Key
Each answer is worth one point.
1. Friday   **2.** 8:00   **3.** Wednesday   **4.** 9:00   **5.** Thursday

— Writing
Answers will vary. See Guidelines, page xvii, for scoring.

Worktext ✪✪

— Listening Answer Key
1. b   **2.** b   **3.** a   4. c   **5.** a

Speaking

Either have students respond to you face to face, or have students record their responses on audiotapes. If administered face to face and learners are unable to respond, do one of the following:

- move to the one-star assessment for Speaking.
- ask more specific questions about the episode, such as

   "What happened when Emery Bradford came to the restaurant?"

   "What did Rosa learn in class?"

See Guidelines, page xiv, for scoring.

Language Structure

Answers may vary; possible answers are provided. See Guidelines, page xvi, for scoring.

1. Why don't you look it up in the dictionary? OR Maybe you should look it up in the dictionary. OR How about looking it up in the dictionary?
2. Why don't you check the batteries? OR Maybe you should check the batteries. OR How about checking the batteries?
3. Why don't you throw it away? OR Maybe you should throw it away. OR How about throwing it away?
4. Why don't you change the channel? OR Maybe you should change the channel. OR How about changing the channel?
5. Why don't you take a walk? OR Maybe you should take a walk. OR How about taking a walk?

Critical Thinking

Answers will vary. See Guidelines, page xx, for scoring.

Reading Answer Key

Each answer is worth one point.

1. 2 hours   **2.** 90 minutes   **3.** 2   **4.** 4 hours   **5.** 3 days

Writing

Answers will vary. See Guidelines, page xviii, for scoring.

Worktext ✪✪✪

Listening Answer Key

1. c   **2.** c   **3.** a   **4.** c   **5.** c

Speaking

Either have students respond to you face to face, or have students record their responses on audiotapes. If administered face to face and learners are unable to respond, do one of the following:

- move to the two-star assessment for Speaking.

- ask more detailed questions such as the following.

    <u>for the meaning of the title</u>
    Who thought that time is money?
    Who learned that teamwork is important?
    How did Mr. Brashov feel about the changes at his restaurant?
    How did the employees feel about the changes?

    <u>for telling the story</u>
    Why did Emery Bradford come to the restaurant?
    Why was there a contest?
    Who won the contest?
    How does Mr. Brashov feel about his employees at the beginning of the episode?
    How does he feel at the end?

Variation: Have learners respond to general statements such as:

Tell about Mr. Brashov's organization problem?
Tell about Emery's ideas and the contest.
Tell about Rosa's experience in class.
Tell what Mr. Brashov thinks about Emery's ideas.

See Guidelines, page xv, for scoring.

Language Structure
Answers may vary; possible answers are provided. See Guidelines, page xvi, for scoring.

1. Why don't you return it? OR Maybe you should return it. OR How about returning it?
2. Why don't you ask him or her to speak more slowly? OR Maybe you should ask him or her to speak more slowly. OR How about asking him or her to speak more slowly?
3. Why don't you look in your coat pocket? OR Maybe you should look in your coat pocket. OR How about looking in your coat pocket?
4. Why don't you get up earlier in the morning? OR Maybe you should get up earlier in the morning. OR How about getting up earlier in the morning?
5. Why don't you check with the payroll office? OR Maybe you should check with the payroll office. OR How about checking with the payroll office?

Critical Thinking
Answers will vary. See Guidelines, page xx, for scoring.

Reading Answer Key
Answer 1 is worth two points; answer 2 is worth three points.

1. No; the classes are at the same time. (one point for each part of the question)
2. Yes; Get Fit Fast classes are Monday, Wednesday, Friday so you can take Cake Decorating or Volleyball; you can only take one of them, though, because the times overlap.

Writing
Answers will vary. See Guidelines, page xix, for scoring.

Photo Stories

EXAMPLE	Mr. Brashov doesn't like paperwork.

1. Mr. Emery Bradford comes to help.
2. The students wrap a box.
3. Rosa can't accept the prize.
4. Emery helps Mr. Brashov.

Worktext All Levels

EXAMPLE	**KATHERINE:**	Mr. Brashov?
	MR. BRASHOV:	Yes, yes, what is it?
	KATHERINE:	You do know this is the second time this week that Henry's been late.
	MR. BRASHOV:	I'll talk to him.
	KATHERINE:	He knows I have to pick up my children after school every afternoon. If he doesn't get here soon, I'll be late.
	MR. BRASHOV:	Why don't you go, Katherine? I can finish.
	KATHERINE:	Mr. Brashov, you have enough to do. It's Henry's job. He should be here.
	MR. BRASHOV:	You are right. It is his job. But we are like a family here, and if there is a problem, everyone helps.

1.
	JESS:	Here. Let me give you a hand.
	MR. BRASHOV:	The one thing I do not like about having a business is all the paperwork.
	JESS:	Listen—my son has a friend who was the number one student in his business school. Maybe he could help you get organized.
	MR. BRASHOV:	I doubt it.
	JESS:	You really should meet this guy.
	MR. BRASHOV:	Jess . . . what are you looking for?
	JESS:	I think he gave me his business card. Look . . . it's your lucky day.
	MR. BRASHOV:	I do not need any more luck today.
	JESS:	Just keep it in case you change your mind.
	MR. BRASHOV:	I have enough paper already. I appreciate what you are trying to do, but I . . .

2. **MR. BRASHOV:** Emery . . . Emery. Do you really think all this running around is going to be good for my business?

   EMERY: Absolutely. Look how fast all your people are working.

   MR. BRASHOV: But the question is how long can they keep it up?

   EMERY: They all want to win the contest as the most efficient employee at Crossroads Café. Believe me. That will keep them going.

   MR. BRASHOV: I know this contest you set up is a good idea, but I am not so sure I can afford to pay the hundred dollar prize.

   EMERY: Mr. Brashov—an investment in your people . . . is an investment in your future.

3. **JAMAL:** Mr. Brashov, can you get along without me for a few minutes?

   MR. BRASHOV: We will try, Jamal. Where are you going?

   JAMAL: To Bidwell's Hardware Store. I need a new filter for the air conditioner in your office.

   MR. BRASHOV: Jamal, wait a minute. Why aren't you going to Joe's Hardware?

   JAMAL: The filters are cheaper at Bidwell's.

   MR. BRASHOV: How do you know?

   JAMAL: I called all the stores in the telephone book to compare prices, the way Emery said we should.

   MR. BRASHOV: Yeah, but Joe is our neighbor. We always shop there.

   JAMAL: I know, but Bidwell's isn't very far away, and they sell the filters I need for ten cents less than they do at Joe's.

   EMERY: Good work, Jamal. That was the right thing to do.

   MR. BRASHOV: Is saving ten cents more important than a friendship with our neighbor?

   EMERY: At home, maybe not. But here at your business, it is more important.

4. **TEACHER:** So, how are you doing with your paper?

   ROSA: Pretty well.

   TEACHER: Good, good . . . Did you register for next semester yet?

   ROSA: No. I don't know if I'm going to take any more classes.

   TEACHER: Oh really? Why?

   ROSA: I just . . . I'm not sure I'm ever going to be a good manager.

   TEACHER: What makes you say that Rosa?

   ROSA: I did such a terrible job in class last week. Some of the other students are still not speaking to me.

   TEACHER: I'm sure they'll get over it. What's more important, Rosa, is that you learn from the experience.

   ROSA: You mean what not to do?

   TEACHER: No . . . just that sometimes being a good manager means being part of a team . . . whether it's running a business . . . or moving furniture.

5. **KATHERINE:** Wait a minute. There has to be a winner.

   MR. BRASHOV: And there is. My friends . . . the real winner here is Crossroads Café. But the person who deserves this prize . . . is Emery Bradford.

   EMERY: Me? I don't understand.

   MR. BRASHOV: My good friend, Emery, . . . you have done something very special for this restaurant.

   EMERY: Thank you, Mr. Brashov.

   MR. BRASHOV: And now you can use your skills and your talents at some other business that . . .

   EMERY: But Mr. Brashov, there is still so much more to do right here . . .

   MR. BRASHOV: And we will do it! We will take what you have given us and continue.

   EMERY: But I . . . I . . . I

   MR. BRASHOV: You have done enough . . . so from all of us at Crossroads Café . . . thank you . . . and good-bye.

7

Name _____ Date _____

Listening Look at each picture. Listen to the tape. Write the letter of the correct picture on the line.

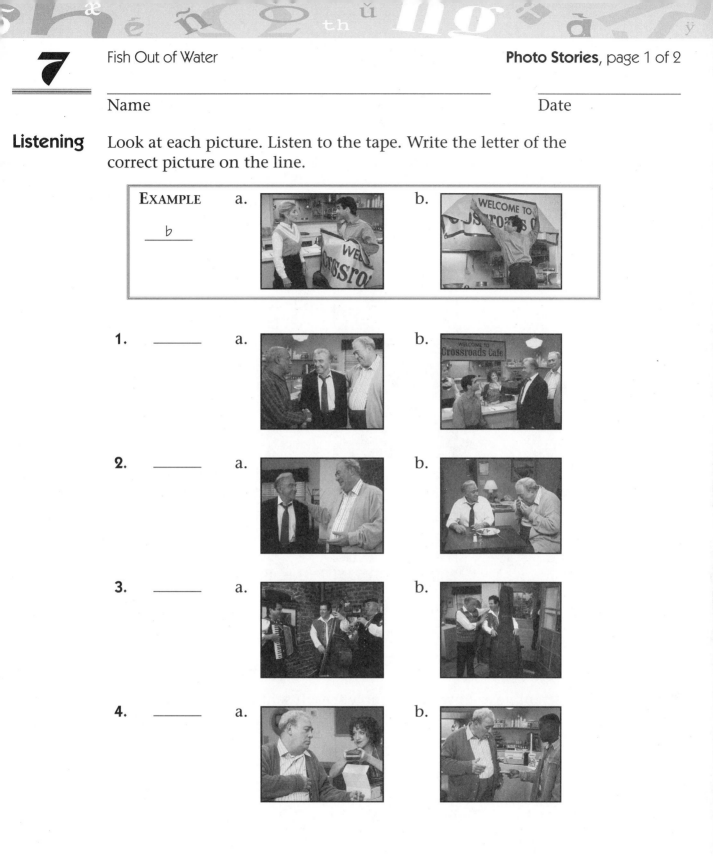

Speaking How are Mr. Brashov and his brother, Nicolae, different? Think about your answer. Tell as much as you can. Your teacher will listen.

Reading   Look at each picture. Choose a, b, or c. Write the letter on the line.

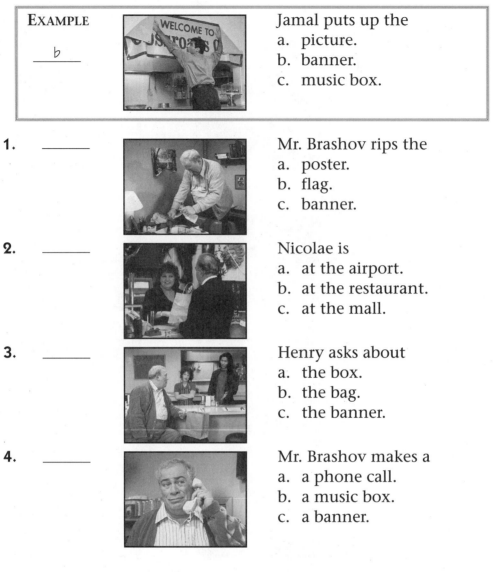

EXAMPLE

___b___

Jamal puts up the
a. picture.
b. banner.
c. music box.

1. _____

Mr. Brashov rips the
a. poster.
b. flag.
c. banner.

2. _____

Nicolae is
a. at the airport.
b. at the restaurant.
c. at the mall.

3. _____

Henry asks about
a. the box.
b. the bag.
c. the banner.

4. _____

Mr. Brashov makes a
a. a phone call.
b. a music box.
c. a banner.

Writing   Unscramble each word. Complete each sentence.

EXAMPLE   Jamal puts up the _b_ _a_ _n_ _n_ _e_ _r_.

(a n e r n b)

1. Nicolae goes to the shopping ___ ___ ___ ___. (a l m l)

2. Mr. Brashov and his brother are business
___ ___ ___ ___ ___ ___ ___ ___. (r p a n e t r s)

3. Nicolae gives his brother a ___ ___ ___ ___ ___ box. (c m i u s)

4. Mr. Brashov shows Rosa a ___ ___ ___ ___ ___ ___ ___ in the
wallet. (e p r i u c t)

7

Name _____   Date _____

Listening   Read each question. Watch the videotape. Circle the letter of the correct answer.

EXAMPLE	How does Nicolae feel?
	(a.) hesitant
	b. confident
	c. impatient

---

1. What are Mr. Brashov and Nicolae talking about?
   a. Romanian food
   b. Romanian language
   c. Romanian people

2. What are Mr. Brashov and Nicolae discussing?
   a. food supplies
   b. letters
   c. recipes

3. What is Nicolae telling Mr. Brashov to do?
   a. take a break
   b. take medicine
   c. take responsibility

4. How does Nicolae feel?
   a. hurt
   b. lonely
   c. worried

5. How does Mr. Brashov feel?
   a. angry
   b. nervous
   c. disappointed

Speaking   Talk about this picture. Tell as much as you can. Your teacher will listen.

Language Structure Talk about experiences.

EXAMPLE	What have you learned?
	I have _learned English._

1. What languages have you studied?

   I have _____

2. Where have you lived?

   I have _____

3. Where have you worked?

   I have _____

4. What has Nicolae done to Crossroads Café?

   He has _____

5. What has Jamal repaired in the café?

   He has _____

Critical Thinking Think about the question below. Write your ideas. Then talk about your ideas. Your teacher will listen.

Do you think Nicolae feels lost in the United States? Tell why or why not.

_____

_____

_____

_____

_____

_____

_____

_____

_____

Name _____   Date _____

Listening   Read each question. Watch the videotape. Circle the letter of the correct answer.

EXAMPLE	How much experience does Nicolae have?
	(a.) as much as Mr. Brashov
	b. less than Mr. Brashov
	c. more than Mr. Brashov

1. Why isn't Mr. Brashov speaking Romanian?
   a. He forgets some of his Romanian.
   b. He refuses to speak any Romanian.
   c. He never learned how to speak Romanian.

2. What does Nicolae want at the restaurant?
   a. Romanian food
   b. Romanian furniture
   c. Romanian workers

3. What is Nicolae's advice?
   a. Mr. Brashov should work more.
   b. Mr. Brashov should relax more.
   c. Mr. Brashov should make more money.

4. What does Nicolae think?
   a. Mr. Brashov should remember his culture.
   b. Mr. Brashov should forget his culture.
   c. Mr. Brashov should change his culture.

5. How does Rosa feel about living in the United States?
   a. She always wants to return to Mexico.
   b. She often wants to return to Mexico.
   c. She never wants to return to Mexico.

Speaking   In this episode, Nicolae makes some changes in the restaurant. He wants to feel like he's in Romania. He wants to speak Romanian, eat Romanian food, and hear Romanian music. Mr. Brashov doesn't want these changes. He doesn't speak much Romanian anymore, and he doesn't want the restaurant to look Romanian. What do you think? Tell as much as you can. Your teacher will listen.

Language Structure   Talk about experiences.

EXAMPLE	What have you done to my restaurant?
	I have tried to make the café more like home.

1. How long have you lived in the United States?

_____

2. What places in the United States have you visited?

_____

3. What languages have you learned?

_____

4. Who has talked with you in English today?

_____

5. What homework have you done today?

_____

Critical Thinking   Think about the question below. Write your ideas. Then talk about your ideas. Your teacher will listen.

Do you think it is hard to live in a new country at first? Tell why or why not.

_____

_____

_____

_____

_____

_____

_____

_____

_____

_____

7

Name _____   Date _____

Listening   Read each question. Watch the videotape. Circle the letter of the correct answer.

EXAMPLE	How does Nicolae feel?

ⓐ He wants to know more about the business.
b. He wants to make more money.
c. He doesn't want to be a partner.

1. What does Nicolae think?
   a. Mr. Brashov should speak more English.
   b. Mr. Brashov should speak more Romanian.
   c. Mr. Brashov should forget Romanian.

2. What does Mr. Brashov think?
   a. Nicolae already understands things here.
   b. Nicolae will never understand things here.
   c. Nicolae will eventually understand things here.

3. What does Mr. Brashov think?
   a. He has forgotten how to ride a bicycle.
   b. He doesn't have time to ride a bicycle.
   c. Riding a bicycle will help him lose weight.

4. How does Mr. Brashov feel?
   a. The United States is his home now.
   b. Romania will always be his home.
   c. He has no home now.

5. Why does Nicolae leave?
   a. He wants his own business.
   b. He doesn't want to work in a restaurant.
   c. The United States is too different from Romania.

Speaking   Explain the title, "Fish Out of Water," or tell the story. Tell as much as you can. Your teacher will listen.

Language Structure   Talk about experiences.

EXAMPLE	What have you done to my restaurant?
	I have tried to make the café more like home.

1. How long have you lived in the United States?

   _____

2. What kind of work experience have you had?

   _____

3. What have you tried to do to feel at home in the United States?

   _____

4. What have you learned about daily life in the United States?

   _____

5. Write a question asking your friend about her or his experiences at work.

   _____

Critical Thinking   Think about the question below. Write your ideas. Then talk about your ideas. Your teacher will listen.

Do you agree that life in the United States is work, work, work? Tell why or why not.

_____

_____

_____

_____

_____

_____

_____

_____

7

Name _____   Date _____

Reading   Read the recipe. Answer the questions.

A Recipe From My Kitchen

Basic Vegetable Soup
Makes 3 quarts

Ingredients
- 2 Tbsp. olive oil
- 2 cups chopped onions
- 1 tsp. minced garlic
- 2 cups peeled, chopped tomatoes
- 1 cup finely sliced carrots
- 1 cup finely sliced celery
- 1 cup cooked, white kidney beans
- 8 cups chicken broth
- 1 1/2 cups diced zucchini
- 1 1/2 cups finely sliced cabbage
- 2 Tbsp. chopped fresh herbs, such as basil or parsley
- Salt and freshly ground pepper (to taste)

🍲 SOUP

Method
1. Heat olive oil and cook the onions for about 10 minutes or until soft.
2. Add the garlic and cook for 30 seconds.
3. Add the tomatoes, carrots, celery, and broth.
4. Bring to boil, reduce heat, and cook gently for about 10 minutes.
5. Add the beans, zucchini, and cabbage.
6. Cook everything for about 15 more minutes.
7. Stir in the herbs.
8. Season with salt and pepper.

✪ 1. What is the name of this dish? _____

2. How many quarts does the recipe make? _____

3. What kind of broth do you use? _____

4. How many cups of chopped tomatoes do you use? _____

5. What kind of oil do you use? _____

✪✪ 1. How many ingredients do you need? _____

2. What do you do after you cook the onions? _____

3. What herbs are suggested? _____

4. How much salt and pepper do you use? _____

5. How long does it take to cook the dish? _____

✪✪✪ 1. Are the ingredients for this dish hard to find? Tell why or why not.

_____

2. Can you make changes in the recipe? Tell why or why not.

_____

3. Is this dish easy to cook? Tell why or why not.

_____

Writing   In this episode, Mr. Brashov's brother, Nicolae, visited the United States. You are Nicolae. Write a postcard to a friend in Romania. Tell about your experiences in the United States.

Learner Checklist

1. Rate yourself.

I CAN . . .	ALWAYS	SOMETIMES	NEVER
talk about experiences.	❏	❏	❏
read a recipe.	❏	❏	❏
write a postcard.	❏	❏	❏
talk about adjusting to a new culture.	❏	❏	❏

2. Meet with your teacher. Talk about how successful you were in reaching the goals for this unit. Compare how you rated yourself with how your teacher rated you.

3. Think about your rating and your teacher's rating. What do you need to study more?

_____

_____

_____

fold -- fold

Instructor Checklist

1. Rate the learner. For each item, circle a number based on the following scale:

3 = easily understood, 2 = understood with difficulty, 1 = not understood

THE LEARNER CAN . . .	RATING	COMMENTS
talk about experiences.	1 2 3	
read a recipe.	1 2 3	
write a postcard.	1 2 3	
talk about adjusting to a new culture.	1 2 3	

2. Meet with the learner. Use the two completed checklists to talk about learner outcomes in this unit and priorities for further study.

Crossroads Café Assessment A

Photo Stories

— Listening Answer Key
1. a   **2.** b   **3.** a   **4.** b

— Speaking
Either have students respond to you face to face, or have students record their responses on audiotapes. See Guidelines, page xii, for scoring.

— Reading Answer Key
1. a   **2.** c   **3.** b   **4.** a

— Writing Answer Key
1. mall   **2.** partner   **3.** music   **4.** picture

Worktext ✪

— Listening Answer Key
1. b   **2.** c   **3.** a   **4.** a   **5.** c

— Speaking
Either have students respond to you face to face, or have students record their responses on audiotapes. See Guidelines, page xiii, for scoring.

— Language Structure
Answers will vary. See Guidelines, page xvi, for scoring.
1. studied English (language)
2. lived in (city)
3. worked at/in (place)
4. worked hard to make it Romanian/changed it
5. repaired the coffee pot/oven/window

— Critical Thinking
Answers will vary. See Guidelines, page xx, for scoring.

— Reading
Each answer is worth one point.
1. Basic Vegetable Soup   **2.** three   **3.** chicken   **4.** two   **5.** olive

— Writing
Answers will vary. See Guidelines, page xvii, for scoring.

Worktext ✪✪

— Listening Answer Key

1. a   **2.** a   **3.** b   **4.** a   **5.** b

— Speaking

Either have students respond to you face to face, or have students record their responses on audiotapes. If administered face to face and learners are unable to respond, do one of the following:

- move to the one-star assessment for Speaking.
- ask more specific questions about the episode, such as

  "What happened when Nicolae put up Romanian decorations and brought in Romanian musicians. How did Mr. Brashov feel? What did he say?"
  OR
  "Why did Nicolae go back to Romania?"

Variation: Ask questions about pictures in Before You Watch (p. 86). Point to each picture and ask questions. For example, picture #4, "What happened when Nicolae took charge of the restaurant?" picture #5, "How did the two brothers feel?"
See Guidelines, page xiv, for scoring.

— Language Structure

Answers will vary; possible answers are provided. See Guidelines, page xvi, for scoring.

1. I have (I've) lived in the United States for *x* years.
2. I have (I've) visited _____.
3. I have (I've) learned *name of language*.
4. My friend/my teacher has talked with me today in English.
5. I have (I've) done my English homework.

— Critical Thinking

Answers will vary. See Guidelines, page xx, for scoring.

— Reading

Each answer is worth one point.

1. twelve
2. add the garlic (and cook for 30 seconds)
3. basil or parsley
4. to taste
5. $35\frac{1}{2}$ minutes or about 35 minutes

— Writing

See Guidelines, page xviii, for scoring.

Worktext ✪✪✪

Listening Answer Key
1. b   **2.** c   **3.** b   **4.** a   **5.** c

Speaking
Either have students respond to you face to face, or have students record their responses on audiotapes. If administered face to face and learners are unable to respond, do one of the following:

- move to the two-star assessment for Speaking.
- ask more detailed questions, such as:

  for the meaning of the title
    Who is the fish out of water?
    Why does Nicolae feel uncomfortable in the United States?
    How does Mr. Brashov feel about his culture?

  for telling the story
    Who came to visit Mr. Brashov?
    What happens when Mr. Brashov stays home sick?
    How does Mr. Brashov feel when he returns?
    What do the two brothers argue about?
    What happens to Nicolae when he goes shopping?
    What does Nicolae decide to do at the end?
    How does Mr. Brashov feel about his brother leaving?

Variation: Have learners respond to general statements such as the following.

  Tell me about Nicolae's visit.
  Tell me about how the two brothers are different.
  Tell me about how the two brothers resolve their differences.

See Guidelines, page xv, for scoring.

Language Structure
Answers will vary; possible answers are provided. See Guidelines, page xvi, for scoring.

1. I have (I've) lived in the United States for <u>x</u> years.
2. I have had factory experience/I have worked in a factory.
3. I have tried to meet people/make friends/learn English.
4. I have learned (that) it is difficult.
5. What have you done at work?/What have you learned?/What kind of experience have you had?

Critical Thinking
Answers will vary. See Guidelines, page xx, for scoring.

— Reading

Answers 1 and 2 are worth two points each; answer 3 is worth one point.
Answers will vary.

1. No, they are easy to find. I have seen these ingredients in the grocery store many times.
2. Yes. If you do not have all the vegetables, it's OK. You can use other ingredients or vegetables.
3. Yes, because you cook everything together in a few minutes. OR No, because there are many ingredients and a lot of chopping.

— Writing

See Guidelines, page xix, for scoring.

Photo Stories

EXAMPLE	Jamal puts up the banner.

1. Nicolae meets Jess.
2. Mr. Brashov has the flu.
3. The band is playing.
4. A man gives the wallet to Mr. Brashov.

Worktext All Levels

EXAMPLE	NICOLAE:	Everything here is just the way you said it would be.
	MR. BRASHOV:	Of course it is. I would never lie to my new partner.
	NICOLAE:	Maybe I should be only a half partner . . . until I know more about the business.
	MR. BRASHOV:	Nonsense. You have had more experience than I have had. (to others) Nicolae is the manager of . . .
	NICOLAE:	. . . Was the manager. . .
	MR. BRASHOV:	. . . Was the manager of a large hotel resort on the Black Sea coast.

1. NICOLAE: Victor, (says something in Romanian about how good the food was).

   MR. BRASHOV: Nicolae, please. My Romanian is not what it used to be.

   NICOLAE: How can you forget your own language?

   MR. BRASHOV: With Eva gone, I have no one to talk to.

   NICOLAE: You should have brought me over before you became so American.

2. NICOLAE: That reminds me. I have a surprise for you.

   MR. BRASHOV: A surprise?

   NICOLAE: Yeah. These are more recipes from home. Now we can give these Americans a real taste of Romania.

   MR. BRASHOV: Yes.

   NICOLAE: I'm sorry, Victor. It was a stupid idea.

   MR. BRASHOV: No, not at all. It is just that things are a little different here. Once you get used to the café, it will all make sense.

   NICOLAE: Of course. I want to learn everything about what you've done.

3. **NICOLAE:** We should take a ride together some time.

   MR. BRASHOV: My bicycle riding days are over. Besides, who has time for such things?

   NICOLAE: Your life can not always be work, work, work. Right, Jess?

   JESS: I keep telling Victor to take a break from this place for a few days.

   MR. BRASHOV: When Crossroads Café takes a break, I will take a break.

4. **NICOLAE:** Victor, I was trying to make it more like home. I thought it would please you.

   MR. BRASHOV: My home is here, in this country.

   NICOLAE: Living here doesn't mean destroying who we are.

   MR. BRASHOV: I am the same person I always was.

   NICOLAE: No, you are not. You are ashamed of where you come from. You are ashamed of our customs, of our language. You are ashamed of me.

   MR. BRASHOV: I will not talk about this anymore.

   NICOLAE: I don't know what has happened to you, Victor. But it breaks my heart. . . . It breaks my heart. I don't want it to happen to me.

5. **MR. BRASHOV:** In another twelve hours Nicolae will be back in Romania. He wouldn't even let me wait until the plane took off. He said he needed to be alone.

   JAMAL: Maybe it's for the best.

   MR. BRASHOV: How can that be possible? This is the United States of America. This could have been his home.

   ROSA: Mr. Brashov, I've been here for five years and it never feels like home.

   MR. BRASHOV: But I thought you were happy here?

   ROSA: Most of the time, I am happy. But sometimes it hurts so much to be away from my family, my friends, my language.

   JAMAL: Change is not for everyone.

8

Name _____   Date _____

Listening   Look at each picture. Listen to the tape. Write the letter of the correct picture on the line.

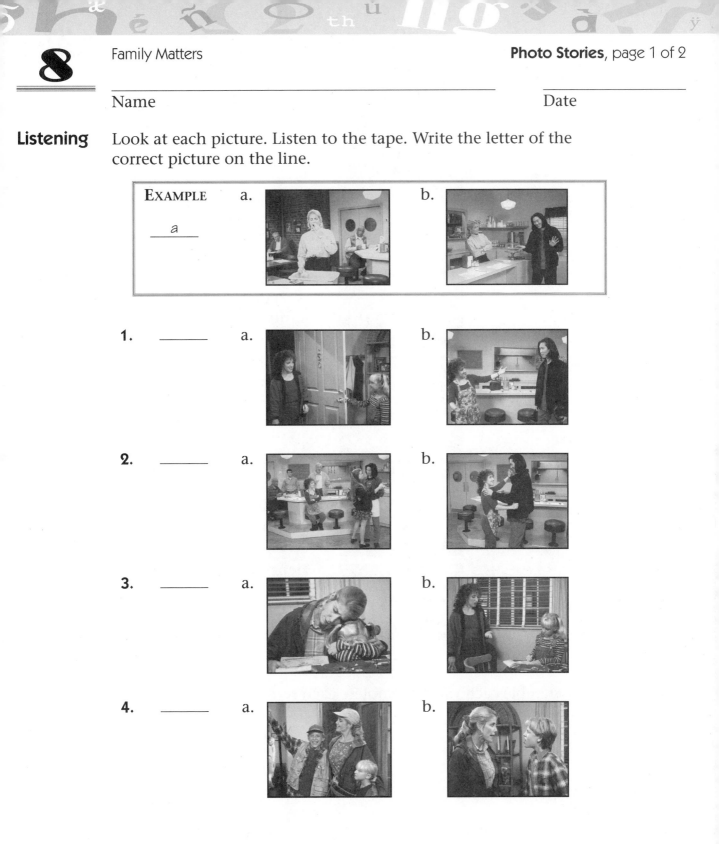

EXAMPLE   a.   b.

_a_

1. _____   a.   b.

2. _____   a.   b.

3. _____   a.   b.

4. _____   a.   b.

Speaking   What does Katherine learn about her family? Think about your answer. Tell as much as you can. Your teacher will listen.

Reading   Look at each picture. Choose a, b, or c. Write the letter on the line.

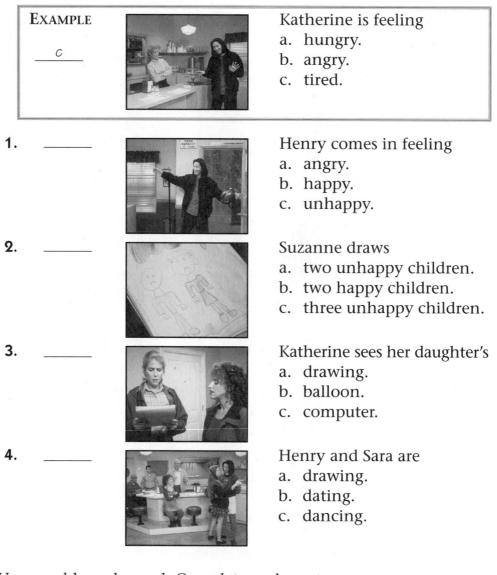

EXAMPLE

_c_

Katherine is feeling
a. hungry.
b. angry.
c. tired.

1. _____

Henry comes in feeling
a. angry.
b. happy.
c. unhappy.

2. _____

Suzanne draws
a. two unhappy children.
b. two happy children.
c. three unhappy children.

3. _____

Katherine sees her daughter's
a. drawing.
b. balloon.
c. computer.

4. _____

Henry and Sara are
a. drawing.
b. dating.
c. dancing.

Writing   Unscramble each word. Complete each sentence.

EXAMPLE   Katherine is _t_ _i_ _r_ _e_ _d_. (i e d r t)

1. Katherine is a single mother, she is ___ ___ ___ ___ ___ ___ ___ ___.
   (d v r c o i d e)

2. Rosa teaches Henry how to ___ ___ ___ ___ ___. (a c e n d)

3. Katherine wants to buy a ___ ___ ___ ___ ___ ___ ___ ___ for
   David to help with his school work. (o p t e u m r c)

4. Katherine thinks David ___ ___ ___   ___ ___ ___ ___ from home
   because he was unhappy. (n a r   w a a y)

_____   _____
Name   Date

Listening   Read each question. Watch the videotape. Circle the letter of the correct answer.

> **EXAMPLE**   Who wants to buy a computer?
> a. Mr. Brashov
> ⓑ Katherine
> c. Jamal

1. How does Henry feel about the dance?
a. excited
b. glad
c. unhappy

2. How does Katherine feel?
a. worried
b. excited
c. impatient

3. How does Katherine feel about Rosa's visit?
a. surprised and angry
b. surprised and glad
c. surprised and sad

4. Why does Katherine have to leave?
a. She needs to take her children to school.
b. She needs to call her children's father.
c. She needs to find her children.

5. What was Rosa teaching Henry?
a. how to dance
b. how to cook
c. how to drive

Speaking   Talk about this picture. Tell as much as you can. Your teacher will listen.

Language Structure Make offers.

EXAMPLE	I'm thirsty.
	I'll get you _something to drink._

1. I can't drive.

   I'll _____

2. This box is too heavy for me to lift.

   I'll _____

3. I need change for a dollar.

   I'll _____

4. I can't read these directions.

   I'll _____

5. I don't know how to sew.

   I'll _____

Critical Thinking Think about the question below. Write your ideas. Then talk about your ideas. Your teacher will listen.

Katherine took a second job to buy David a computer. Did she do the right thing? Tell why or why not.

_____

_____

_____

_____

_____

_____

_____

_____

_____

_____

_____   _____
Name   Date

Listening Read each question. Watch the videotape. Circle the letter of the correct answer.

EXAMPLE	What does Jamal offer to do? a. help Mr. Brashov choose a computer (b.) help Katherine choose a computer c. help both of them choose a computer

1. Why does Henry say he has to get back to work?
    a. Mr. Brashov will fire him.
    b. Mr. Brashov will get angry.
    c. Mr. Brashov will give him some work.

2. What does the woman finally want?
    a. the meat loaf
    b. the tuna
    c. another restaurant

3. What does Rosa say?
    a. She was worried because Katherine has been so tired.
    b. She was worried because Katherine has been so angry.
    c. She was worried because Katherine has been so strange.

4. What does Katherine say to Rosa?
    a. David's father has deserted them.
    b. David's father has blamed Katherine.
    c. David's father has hurt him.

5. Why does Sara come to the restaurant?
    a. to talk to Henry about Rosa
    b. to talk to Rosa about Henry
    c. to talk to Henry about the dance

Speaking In this episode, Katherine has some problems with her children. She is tired because she's working two jobs. It's not easy to be a single parent. What should Katherine do? Do you know any parents who are single? What kinds of problems do they have? How do they solve them? Tell as much as you can. Your teacher will listen.

Language Structure Make offers.

EXAMPLE	I want to look for a larger apartment.
	I'll help you look.
	OR
	Would you like me to help you look?

1. I have to paint the living room.

   _____

2. I want to make a salad for dinner tonight.

   _____

3. I can't open this jar.

   _____

4. I don't feel like cooking tonight.

   _____

5. This soup is too cold.

   _____

Critical Thinking Think about the question below. Write your ideas. Then talk about your ideas. Your teacher will listen.

Do you think it is important for parents to spend time with their children? Tell why or why not.

_____

_____

_____

_____

_____

_____

_____

Family Matters

Name _____   Date _____

Listening   Read each question. Watch the videotape. Circle the letter of the correct answer.

> **EXAMPLE**   What does Jamal think of the computer in the ad?
> a. It will be outdated in 5 years.
> b. It is outdated already.
> c. It will be outdated in a few years.

1. Why does Henry want Sara to leave?
    a. because he's busy and has work to do
    b. because he's embarrassed and uncomfortable
    c. because he's afraid of Mr. Brashov

2. What does the woman think?
    a. Rosa is not a good cook because the food is too heavy and not fresh.
    b. Katherine is not a good waitress because she doesn't have good suggestions.
    c. Katherine is not a good waitress because she is in a hurry.

3. Why does Rosa really visit Katherine?
    a. She wanted to bring Katherine some nylons.
    b. She wanted to see how Katherine is feeling.
    c. She wanted to see how Suzanne is feeling.

4. Why is Katherine worried?
    a. She thinks her children have run away.
    b. She thinks her children are lost.
    c. She thinks her children are with their father.

5. Why was Sara upset?
    a. She was jealous of Rosa.
    b. She was afraid of Rosa.
    c. She was angry at Rosa.

Speaking   Explain the title, "Family Matters," or tell the story. Tell as much as you can. Your teacher will listen.

Language Structure   Make offers.

EXAMPLE	I'm going shopping at the mall.
	I'll go shopping with you.
	OR
	Would you like me to go shopping with you?

1. I can't go to English class tonight. My car is at the repair shop.

   _____

2. I can't find Elm Street on this map.

   _____

3. My baby-sitter is sick today.

   _____

4. I need to mail these bills.

   _____

5. This coffee is too cold to drink.

   _____

Critical Thinking   Think about the question below. Write your ideas. Then talk about your ideas. Your teacher will listen.

Which matters more to you—having a happy family life or having many possessions? Tell why.

_____

_____

_____

_____

_____

_____

_____

_____

Name

Date

Reading Read the following product advertisement. Answer the questions.

A

Free Monitor
with the purchase of this computer

120 MHz Intel Pentium Processor

- 16 MB RAM expandable to 128 MB
- 1.06 GB hard drive
- 14.4K fax/data modem
- 4X CD-ROM drive

$1099 Everyday Low Price

B

Pentium 100
Multimedia Computer
with 14-inch Color Monitor

Value-priced package featuring advanced Pentium 100 MHz performance! Includes 100 MHz Intel Pentium Processor, 8 MB RAM memory, 1.0 GB hard disk drive, quad speed CD-ROM drive and 14.4 kbps fax modem

Everyday Price — **$1,198**

✪ 1. What is the price of computer A? _____

 2. How many MHz does computer A have? _____

 3. What size is computer B's monitor? _____

✪✪ 1. Which computer costs more? _____

 2. Which computer has more MHz? _____

 3. Which computer has fax ability? _____

 4. Which computer has a color monitor? _____

 5. What size is the hard drive of computer A? _____

✪✪✪ 1. Compare ads A and B. Which components are the same? _____

_____

 2. Compare ads A and B. Which components are different? _____

_____

 3. Which computer is the better buy? Tell why. _____

_____

Writing Write about Katherine's decision to take a second job. Do you think it was a good decision or a bad decision? Give three reasons for your opinion.

Learner Checklist

1. Rate yourself.

I CAN . . .	ALWAYS	SOMETIMES	NEVER
make offers.	❑	❑	❑
read product ads.	❑	❑	❑
write about a bad decision.	❑	❑	❑
talk about the problems of single parenting.	❑	❑	❑

2. Meet with your teacher. Talk about how successful you were in reaching the goals for this unit. Compare how you rated yourself with how your teacher rated you.

3. Think about your rating and your teacher's rating. What do you need to study more?

_____

_____

_____

fold - fold

Instructor Checklist

1. Rate the learner. For each item, circle a number based on the following scale:

3 = easily understood, 2 = understood with difficulty, 1 = not understood

THE LEARNER CAN . . .	RATING	COMMENTS
make offers.	1　2　3	
read product ads.	1　2　3	
write about a bad decision.	1　2　3	
talk about the problems of single parenting.	1　2　3	

2. Meet with the learner. Use the two completed checklists to talk about learner outcomes in this unit and priorities for further study.

Photo Stories

— Listening Answer Key
1. a   **2.** b   **3.** a   **4.** b

— Speaking
Either have students respond to you face to face, or have students record their responses on audiotapes. See Guidelines, page xii, for scoring.

— Reading Answer Key
1. b   **2.** a   **3.** a   **4.** c

— Writing Answer Key
1. divorced   **2.** dance   **3.** computer   **4.** ran away

Worktext ✪

— Listening Answer Key
1. c   **2.** c   **3.** a   **4.** c   **5.** a

— Speaking
Either have students respond to you face to face, or have students record their responses on audiotapes. See Guidelines, page xiii, for scoring.

— Language Structure Answer Key
Answers may vary; possible answers are provided. See Guidelines, page xvi, for scoring.
1. teach you to drive.
2. lift it for you.
3. give you change.
4. give you directions.
5. teach you how to sew.

— Critical Thinking
Answers will vary. See Guidelines, page xx, for scoring.

— Reading Answer Key
Answer 1 is worth one point; answers 2 and 3 are worth two points each.
1. $1099   **2.** 120   **3.** 14 inches

— Writing
Answers will vary. See Guidelines, page xvii, for scoring.

Worktext ✪✪

— Listening Answer Key
1. b   **2.** c   **3.** c   **4.** a   **5.** c

— Speaking

Either have students respond to you face to face, or have students record their responses on audiotapes. If administered face to face and learners are unable to respond, do one of the following:

- move to the one-star assessment for Speaking.
- ask more detailed questions about the episode, such as

  "What happened when Rosa came to Katherine's apartment?"
  OR
  "Why was David upset?"

Variation: Ask questions about pictures in Before You Watch (p. 100). For example, point to picture #4 and ask, "What is Suzanne doing?" "What is she saying to Rosa?"

See Guidelines, page xiv, for scoring.

— Language Structure Answer Key

Answers may vary; possible answers are provided. See Guidelines, page xvi, for scoring.

1. I'll help you paint the living room. OR Would you like me to help you paint the living room?
2. I'll help you make a salad. OR Would you like me to help you make a salad?
3. I'll open the jar for you. OR Would you like me to open the jar for you?
4. I'll cook. OR Would you like me to cook?
5. I'll heat it up. OR Would you like me to get you something else?

— Critical Thinking

Answers will vary. See Guidelines, page xx, for scoring.

— Reading Answer Key

Each answer is worth one point.

1. b **2.** a **3.** both **4.** b **5.** 1.06 GB

— Writing

Answers will vary. See Guidelines, page xiv, for scoring.

Worktext ✪✪✪

— Listening Answer Key

1. b **2.** c **3.** b **4.** a. **5.** a

— Speaking

Either have students respond to you face to face, or have students record their responses on audiotapes. If administered face to face and learners are unable to respond, do one of the following:

- move to the two-star assessment for Speaking.

- ask more detailed questions, such as:

<u>for the meaning of the title</u>

Who has family problems?
Who says that all the workers are like family?
Who needs help?

<u>for telling the story</u>

Why is Katherine so tired?
Why is Henry so happy?
Why is Katherine interested in buying a computer?
What happens when Sara visits Henry at the restaurant?
Why is Rosa worried about Katherine?
What happens when Rosa visits Katherine?
Why is David so angry?
Who helps Henry learn to dance?
Where does Katherine take her children for the weekend?

Variation: Have learners respond to general statements such as the following.

Tell about Katherine's problems.
Tell about Henry and his girlfriend.
Tell about Suzanne's drawing.
Tell how Katherine feels about her children.

See Guidelines, page xv, for scoring.

Language Structure Answer Key

Answers may vary; possible answers are provided. See Guidelines, page xvi, for scoring.

1. I'll give you a ride. OR Would you like me to give you a ride?
2. I'll find it for you. OR Would you like me to find it for you?
3. I'll watch the children for you. OR Would you like me to watch the children for you?
4. I'll mail them for you. OR Would you like me to mail them for you?
5. I'll get you another cup of coffee. OR Would you like me to get you another cup of coffee?

Critical Thinking

See Guidelines, page xx, for scoring.

Reading Answer Key

Answers 1 and 2 are worth one-half point each; answer 3 is worth two and one-half points.

1. Same components are: CD ROM drive, fax/modem.
2. Different components are: MHz, RAM, hard drive.
3. A is the better buy. It is cheaper and it has more MHz (memory), more RAM, and more GB on hard drive.

Writing

See Guidelines, page xix, for scoring.

Photo Stories

EXAMPLE	Katherine is tired.

1. Rosa goes to Katherine's apartment.
2. Rosa dances with Henry.
3. Katherine and Suzanne are unhappy.
4. Katherine and David are angry.

Worktext All Levels

EXAMPLE	KATHERINE:	Jamal, what do you know about computers?
	JAMAL:	I know that they are very expensive and that I can't afford one.
	KATHERINE:	But prices are coming down. Look at this.
	JAMAL:	This is a close-out. It's on sale because it's last year's model.
	KATHERINE:	But it would work, wouldn't it?
	JAMAL:	Sure, but it would be slow. And it might be totally outdated in a couple of years. Are you thinking of buying a computer? I'll be glad to help you choose one.
	KATHERINE:	No . . . I was just curious. That's all.
	JAMAL:	It would be nice to own a computer. But unless Mr. Brashov suddenly decides to give me a raise, it's a luxury I can't afford.
	KATHERINE:	That makes two of us.

1. **SARA:** Aren't you excited about the dance?

   HENRY: Oh, sure.

   SARA: The decorating committee's going to be a lot of work, but we have some really great ideas for the gym. Would you like to help us?

   HENRY: Ah . . . well . . . I'm not very good at that sort of thing.

   SARA: But it wouldn't be that hard. We have . . .

   HENRY: Look, I had better get back to work before Mr. Brashov gets mad at me.

   SARA: He seems like a sweet man.

   HENRY: Yeah, well, you don't know him like I do.

2. KATHERINE: Have you decided yet?

WOMAN CUSTOMER: Not quite. How's the tuna?

KATHERINE: Very good. Made fresh every day.

WOMAN CUSTOMER: I don't know . . . I'm not really in a mood for fish. How's the meat loaf?

KATHERINE: Excellent choice.

WOMAN CUSTOMER: No, I need something lighter. Let me see . . .

KATHERINE: Look, I haven't got all day. Pick something.

WOMAN CUSTOMER: Well, if that's your attitude, I will. Another restaurant.

3. KATHERINE: Rosa. What are you doing here?

ROSA: I was at the Emporium for their sale, and I bought you some nylons. I thought I'd drop them off on my way home.

KATHERINE: Thanks, but I really don't need them.

ROSA: That's OK. I can take them back.

KATHERINE: So what are you really doing here?

ROSA: I was worried about you.

KATHERINE: Worried? Why?

ROSA: Because you've been acting weird.

KATHERINE: I've just been a little tired.

ROSA: Yes, I know.

4. KATHERINE: I have to leave, Mr. Brashov. There's no answer at my apartment. David and Suzanne should have been home from school by now.

JESS: Did you call the school?

KATHERINE: Yes . . . they left almost an hour ago.

ROSA: Where could they go?

KATHERINE: I don't know.

JAMAL: I'm sure they're all right.

KATHERINE: You saw what happened last night. David's still hurting because of the divorce. Their father practically deserted us, and I know David blames me for that.

5. **HENRY:** Sara? What are you doing here?

   SARA: You left a message that you wanted to tell me the truth (indicating Rosa) about her.

   HENRY: Look. It's not what you think. Rosa and I are just friends.

   ROSA: In fact, we are hardly even friends. We just work together.

   SARA: You two seemed pretty friendly to me.

   HENRY: Look Sara. The reason I didn't ask you to the holiday dance was because . . . I can't dance . . . and Rosa was teaching me.

9

Name _____

Date _____

Listening Look at each picture. Listen to the tape. Write the letter of the correct picture on the line.

EXAMPLE   a.   b.

___a___

1. _____   a.   b.

2. _____   a.   b.

3. _____   a.   b.

4. _____   a.   b.

Speaking What is Jamal's problem? Think about your answer. Tell as much as you can. Your teacher will listen.

Crossroads Café Assessment A

Reading   Look at each picture. Choose a, b, or c. Write the letter on the line.

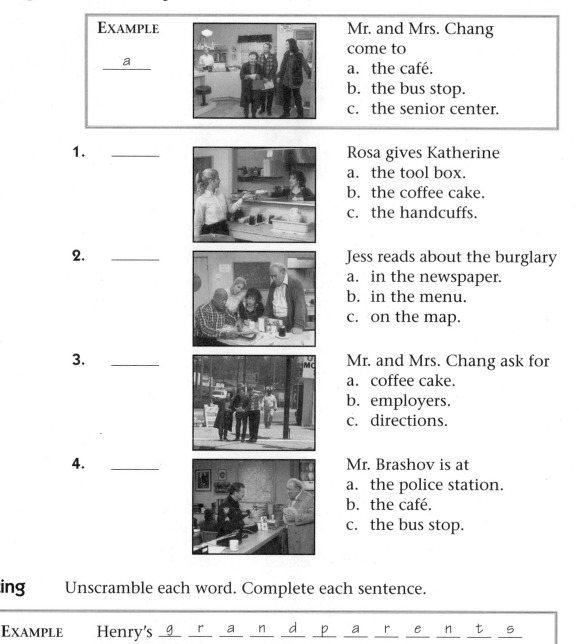

| EXAMPLE _a_ | | Mr. and Mrs. Chang come to
a. the café.
b. the bus stop.
c. the senior center. |

1. _____   Rosa gives Katherine
a. the tool box.
b. the coffee cake.
c. the handcuffs.

2. _____   Jess reads about the burglary
a. in the newspaper.
b. in the menu.
c. on the map.

3. _____   Mr. and Mrs. Chang ask for
a. coffee cake.
b. employers.
c. directions.

4. _____   Mr. Brashov is at
a. the police station.
b. the café.
c. the bus stop.

Writing   Unscramble each word. Complete each sentence.

EXAMPLE   Henry's _g_ _r_ _a_ _n_ _d_ _p_ _a_ _r_ _e_ _n_ _t_ _s_

come to the café. (s g t a r n n e d r a p)

1. Mr. and Mrs. Chang are ___ ___ ___ ___ . They ask for directions.
(t l s o)

2. The police look for a ___ ___ ___ ___ ___ ___ ___ . (b g l r a u r)

3. Jamal is not ___ ___ ___ ___ ___ ___ . He is not the burglar.
(u l y t i g)

4. Mr. Brashov is the ___ ___ ___ ___ ___ ___ ___ ___ of Jamal.
(m l y e o p e r)

9

_____   _____
Name   Date

Listening   Read each question. Watch the videotape. Circle the letter of the correct answer.

EXAMPLE	How do Henry's grandparents feel?
	a. shy
	(b.) afraid
	c. embarrassed

1. How does Jamal feel?
   a. nervous
   b. sad
   c. happy

2. What is Jess reading about in the newspaper?
   a. shootings
   b. kidnappings
   c. burglaries

3. What are the police talking about with Jamal?
   a. his immigration papers
   b. his driver's license
   c. his insurance papers

4. What does Mr. Brashov think about Jamal?
   a. He is a criminal.
   b. He is a good person.
   c. He is a difficult person.

5. What does Mr. Brashov tell the police?
   a. Jamal was at work last night.
   b. Jamal was with his wife last night.
   c. Jamal was at home last night.

Speaking   Talk about this picture. Tell as much as you can. Your teacher will listen.

Language Structure   Describe people.

EXAMPLE	How tall is Rosa?
	She is about five feet tall.

1. How tall is Mr. Brashov?

   He is _____

2. What kind of hair does Katherine have?

   It is _____

3. What kind of hair does your teacher have?

   It is _____

4. What does Jamal look like?

   He is _____

5. What do you look like?

   I am _____

Critical Thinking   Think about the question below. Write your ideas. Then talk about your ideas. Your teacher will listen.

Do you think Jamal was angry with the police officers? Tell why or why not.

_____

_____

_____

_____

_____

_____

_____

_____

_____

Rush to Judgment

Worktext ✪✪, page 1 of 2

Name _____   Date _____

Listening   Read each question. Watch the videotape. Circle the letter of the correct answer.

EXAMPLE	How do Henry's grandparents feel about the police?
	a. They are happy with them.
	(b.) They are afraid of them.
	c. They are angry at them.

1. What do the police want to know about Jamal?
   a. where he is going
   b. where he works
   c. where he was last night

2. What does Jess read about in the newspaper?
   a. Some people saw the burglar.
   b. Some people know the burglar.
   c. Some people caught the burglar.

3. Why can't the police identify Jamal?
   a. They have the wrong name.
   b. They have the wrong country.
   c. They have the wrong language.

4. What is Mr. Brashov trying to say?
   a. Jamal might be guilty.
   b. Jamal can not be innocent.
   c. Jamal can not be guilty.

5. What do the police want to prove?
   a. Jamal's last name is Al-Jibali.
   b. Jamal is an engineer.
   c. Jamal was at home last night.

Speaking   In this episode, the police judged Jamal because of the way he looked. Have you ever judged people because of the way they looked? Has someone ever judged you because of the way you looked? Why does this happen? Tell as much as you can. Your teacher will listen.

©Heinle & Heinle Publishers
Duplication for classroom use is permitted.

Crossroads Café Assessment A

9-5

Language Structure Describe people.

EXAMPLE	What does Jamal look like?
	He has a medium build and dark hair.

1. What does Rosa look like?

   _____

2. What kind of employee is Katherine?

   _____

3. How old is Mr. Brashov?

   _____

4. What kind of hair does Henry have?

   _____

5. What do you look like?

   _____

Critical Thinking Think about the question below. Write your ideas. Then talk about your ideas. Your teacher will listen.

Do you think it is important for people to know the names of the police officers in their communities? Tell why or why not.

_____

_____

_____

_____

_____

_____

_____

_____

_____

9

_____   _____

Name   Date

Listening   Read each question. Watch the videotape. Circle the letter of the correct answer.

> **EXAMPLE**   What does Henry think of the police in the United States?
> a. They are probably better than the police in China.
> b. They are probably as bad as the police in China.
> c. They are probably worse than the police in China.

1. Why does Jamal feel uncomfortable?
    a. because he did nothing wrong
    b. because he did something wrong
    c. because he is hiding his driver's license

2. Why is Jamal at the police station?
    a. He saw the burglar.
    b. He looks like the burglar.
    c. He knows the burglar.

3. How does Jamal feel?
    a. He is afraid because he is illegal.
    b. He is frustrated because he is legal.
    c. He is nervous because he has a false social security number.

4. Why is Mr. Brashov upset?
    a. He knows Jamal is innocent, but he can't prove it.
    b. He knows Jamal is guilty, but he can't prove it.
    c. He knows Jamal is guilty, but he can't believe it.

5. Why don't the police believe what Jamal says?
    a. They need proof that he was at home.
    b. They have proof that he wasn't at home.
    c. They have proof that he did the burglary.

Speaking   Explain the title, "Rush to Judgment," or tell the story. Tell as much as you can. Your teacher will listen.

Language Structure Describe people.

EXAMPLE	What does Mr. Brashov look like?
	<u>He is in his early sixties and has a large build.</u>

1. What does Jamal look like?

   _____

2. What does Henry look like?

   _____

3. What do you look like?

   _____

4. How do you feel after you work hard all day?

   _____

5. Write a question asking your friend about her or his height.

   _____

Critical Thinking Think about the question below. Write your ideas. Then talk about your ideas. Your teacher will listen.

Are the roles of police officers in your country the same as the roles of police officers in the United States? Tell how they are the same or different.

_____

_____

_____

_____

_____

_____

_____

_____

_____   _____
Name   Date

Reading   Read the police report. Answer the questions.

1. DATE: 4/27	2. NAME: (LAST) Granieri	3. (FIRST) Paolo	4. MIDDLE INITIAL: S.	5. GENDER: Male
6. DATE OF BIRTH: 10/28/66		7. DRIVER'S LICENSE #: G222-0555-7777		8. WEAPONS? NO
9. HEIGHT: 5 ft. 9 in.	10. WEIGHT: 170 lbs.	11. HAIR: black, curly		12. BUILD: medium
13. EYES: brown	14. MARKS: 1 scar—right arm between elbow and wrist			15. GLASSES: No
16. COMPLEXION: medium	17. HOME ADDRESS: 250 Glengarry St. Apt. # 7, Westown			18. PHONE NUMBER: 555-6789
19. MARITAL STATUS: Single	20. NAME OF SPOUSE: (LAST) N/A			21. (FIRST) N/A
22. PLACE OF EMPLOYMENT: ChemCo	23. ADDRESS: 1 West 22nd St., Brookville			24. PHONE NUMBER: 555-9762
25. NAME OF EMPLOYER: Ralph Burns	26. OCCUPATION: Chemical researcher			
27. PLACE OF BIRTH: Naples, Italy	28. U.S. CITIZEN? No			29. PERMANENT RESIDENT? Yes
30. PERSON TO CONTACT IN CASE OF EMERGENCY: Anna Bocconi				

Description of incident: We saw Mr. Paolo S. Granieri in his vehicle weaving in and out of the center lane on Main Street. It appeared that the suspect was DUI (Driving Under the Influence). We stopped him for a Breathalizer test to check his blood-alcohol level. The test proved he was drunk. We read Mr. Granieri his rights, took him to the police station, and put him in jail for the night.

Signature: _Detective Brennan_

✪ **1.** Where does Paolo live? _____

2. How much does Paolo weigh? _____

3. What color is his hair? _____

4. Who is the person to contact in an emergency? _____

5. How tall is Paolo? _____

✪✪ **1.** Was Paolo drunk? How do you know? _____

2. Did Paolo have a gun? How do you know? _____

3. Has Paolo lived his entire life in the United States? How do you

know? _____

✪✪✪ **1.** Were the police wrong about the suspect being DUI?   YES   NO

2. Was Paolo arrested? Tell why or why not. _____

_____

3. According to the police report, Paolo was weaving in and out of a lane when he was driving. If his driving had been good, would the police have stopped him? Tell why or why not.

_____

Writing   What do you want to know about your community? Write a letter to someone in your city's government. Request information about services that are important to you.

Learner Checklist

1. Rate yourself.

I CAN . . .	ALWAYS	SOMETIMES	NEVER
describe people.	❑	❑	❑
read a police report.	❑	❑	❑
write a letter requesting information.	❑	❑	❑
talk about roles of police officers.	❑	❑	❑

2. Meet with your teacher. Talk about how successful you were in reaching the goals for this unit. Compare how you rated yourself with how your teacher rated you.

3. Think about your rating and your teacher's rating. What do you need to study more?

_____

_____

_____

fold - fold

Instructor Checklist

1. Rate the learner. For each item, circle a number based on the following scale:

3 = easily understood, 2 = understood with difficulty, 1 = not understood

THE LEARNER CAN . . .	RATING	COMMENTS
describe people.	1 2 3	
read a police report.	1 2 3	
write a letter requesting information.	1 2 3	
talk about roles of police officers.	1 2 3	

2. Meet with the learner. Use the two completed checklists to talk about learner outcomes in this unit and priorities for further study.

Crossroads Café Assessment A

Photo Stories

— Listening Answer Key

1. b   **2.** a   **3.** a   **4.** b

— Speaking

Either have students respond to you face to face, or have students record their responses on audiotapes. See Guidelines, page xii, for scoring.

— Reading Answer Key

1. b   **2.** a   **3.** c   **4.** a

— Writing Answer Key

1. lost   **2.** burglar   **3.** guilty   **4.** employer

Worktext ✪

— Listening Answer Key

1. a   **2.** c   **3.** a   **4.** b   **5.** c

— Speaking

Either have students respond to you face to face, or have students record their responses on audiotapes. See Guidelines, page xiii, for scoring.

— Language Structure

Some answers may vary; possible answers are provided. See Guidelines, page xvi, for scoring.

1. about six feet tall   **2.** long (and blond)   **3.** (hair color, type, and/or length)
4. medium build/about six feet tall with black or dark hair
5. (student's height/build and hair color, type, and/or length)

— Critical Thinking

Answers will vary. See Guidelines, page xx, for scoring.

— Reading Answer Key

Each answer is worth one point.
1. Westown   **2.** 170 lbs.   **3.** black   **4.** Anna Bocconi   **5.** 5 ft. 9 in.

— Writing

Answers will vary. See Guidelines, page xvii, for scoring.

Worktext ✪✪

— Listening Answer Key

1. c   **2.** a   **3.** a   **4.** c   **5.** c

— Speaking

Either have students respond to you face to face, or have students record their responses on audiotapes. If administered face to face and learners are unable to respond, do one of the following:

- move to the one-star assessment for Speaking.
- ask more detailed questions about the episode, such as

  "Why was Jamal stopped by the police?" "What questions did they ask him?" "How did he feel?"

  OR

  "What was Jamal doing at the police station?"

Variation: Ask questions about pictures 1–6 in Before You Watch (p. 86). For example, point to picture #2 and ask: "What is happening to Jamal?" "How does he feel?"

See Guidelines, page xiv, for scoring.

— Language Structure

Answers may vary; possible answers are provided. See Guidelines, page xvi, for scoring.

1. She is short/about five feet tall (with brown and/or curly hair).
2. She is a good/valued employee.
3. He is in his sixties/about sixty-years old.
4. He has straight/black/long hair.
5. I am (student's height/build) with (hair color/type).

— Critical Thinking

Answers will vary. See Guidelines, page xx, for scoring.

— Reading Answer Key

Answers 1 and 3 are worth two points each; answer 2 is worth one point.

1. Yes, he failed the breathalizer test.
2. No, because it says NO after weapons.
3. No, he was born in Italy and he is not a United States citizen.

— Writing

Answers will vary. See Guidelines, page xvii, for scoring.

Worktext ✪✪✪

— Listening Answer Key

1. a   **2.** b   **3.** b   **4.** a   **5.** a

— Speaking

Either have learners respond to you face to face, or have them record their responses on audiotapes. If administered face to face, and learners are unable to respond, do one of the following:

- move to the two-star assessment for Speaking.

- ask more detailed questions, such as the following:

  <u>for the meaning of the title</u>

  Who made rash judgments?
  Why was Jamal brought to the police station?
  How was Jamal treated by the police?
  How did Henry's grandparents feel about police (before and after getting lost)?

  <u>for telling the story</u>

  How did Henry's grandparents react to the police?
  Why were they afraid?
  What happened when Jamal was stopped by police?
  Why didn't he have identification?
  What questions did the police ask Jamal at the station?
  What happened when Mr. Brashov came to help him?
  How did Jamal prove that he was innocent?
  How did Jamal feel after he was set free?
  Who helped return Henry's grandparents to the restaurant?
  How did their attitudes toward police change?

Variation: Have learners respond to general statements such as the following.

Tell about Jamal's interrogation and release.
Tell about Henry's grandparents and their attitudes toward police.
Tell about what judgments people made and about how their judgments changed.

See Guidelines, page xv, for scoring.

Language Structure

Answers may vary; possible answers are provided. See Guidelines, page xvi, for scoring.

1. He is in his late twenties with a medium build.
2. He is about six feet tall with straight black hair.
3. I am (student's height/age/hair).
4. I feel tired.
5. How tall are you?

Critical Thinking

Answers will vary. See Guidelines, page xx, for scoring.

Reading Answer Key

Answer 1 is worth one point; answers 2 and 3 are worth two points each.

1. no
2. Yes, he failed the breathalizer./They read him his rights.
3. No, because he did not look suspicious./The police can not know if someone is drunk if the driving is good.

Writing

Answers will vary. See Guidelines, page xix, for scoring.

Photo Stories

EXAMPLE	Henry brings his grandparents to the café.

1. Jamal picks up his toolbox.
2. The dectective talks to Jamal.
3. Jamal leaves the police station.
4. Grandma and Grandpa Chang thank the police officer.

Worktext, All Levels

EXAMPLE	MR. BRASHOV:	Henry, this is Detective Anderson.
	HENRY:	Oh . . . police.
	DET. ANDERSON:	Nice to meet you.
	DET. BENTON:	Thanks for the coffee cake.
	MR. BRASHOV:	My pleasure.
	MR. BRASHOV:	Is there a problem, Henry?
	HENRY:	My grandparents are just afraid of the police.
	MR. BRASHOV:	Why?
	HENRY:	In China, the police weren't very nice to them. And from the stories I've heard, they're not so nice here, either.

1. **DET. ANDERSON:** Can I see some identification?

    JAMAL: All right. My driver's license is in my wallet. I always carry it in my back pocket. It should be here. I guess I was so tired this morning, I just forgot to take it with me. Our baby has been sick. She kept us up most of the night.

    DET. ANDERSON: What's your name, pal?

    JAMAL: Jamal Al-Jibali

    DET. ANDERSON: Where were you last night around eleven-thirty?

    JAMAL: At home with my wife and daughter. As I told you, my baby was sick. I don't understand. Is it against the law to not have identification?

2. MR. BRASHOV: The police took Jamal to the station.

ROSA: Why?

MR. BRASHOV: To question him.

KATHERINE: About what?

MR. BRASHOV: I couldn't understand everything. He spoke so fast. Something about burglaries.

JESS: Wait a minute. I read something in the Metro section. Here it is. Wanted in a string of recent burglaries . . . eyewitnesses describe the suspect as being male, medium build, late twenties, possibly of Middle Eastern origin.

KATHERINE: Oh—don't tell me the police think Jamal is involved.

3. DET. BENTON: This just came in from the Immigration Service.

DET. ANDERSON: So what's the story?

DET. BENTON: They still can't seem to identify him.

JAMAL: That's impossible. May I take a look?

DET. ANDERSON: Be my guest.

JAMAL: May I borrow your pen, please. My last name is "Al-Jibali." You have, "Jihali."

DET. BENTON: Oh, OK . . . I'll . . . Uh . . . try it again.

JAMAL: You see? You've got the wrong man.

4. MR. BRASHOV: I'm here to see Jamal Al-Jibali. I am Victor Brashov, his employer.

SELTZER: He's being questioned.

MR. BRASHOV: Why? What has Jamal done?

SELTZER: He's a possible suspect.

MR. BRASHOV: Listen, you do not know Jamal. I would swear my life on his good name.

SELTZER: I appreciate what you're saying. Now why don't you just have a seat and relax.

MR. BRASHOV: Jamal is not a criminal.

SELTZER: Hey, have a seat or you'll have to wait outside.

5. **DET. BENTON:** "Jamal Al-Jibali. Occupation, engineer. Wife, Jihan El Bially." It's all here.

DET. ANDERSON: Yeah, but it doesn't mean a thing. He still could have done the burglary.

JAMAL: But I was home last night.

DET. ANDERSON: Right now, all we have is your word for that and I'm afraid that's just not good enough.

MR. BRASHOV: Wait a minute! Jamal called me last night.

DET. BENTON: What time?

MR. BRASHOV: It must have been around eleven-thirty. I remember because I had just finished watching the news.

_____   _____
Name   Date

Listening   Look at each picture. Listen to the tape. Write the letter of the correct picture on the line.

EXAMPLE   a.   b.

     _a_

1. _____   a.   b.

2. _____   a.   b.

3. _____   a.   b.

4. _____   a.   b.

Speaking   What does Barbara want from Mr. Brashov? Think about your answer. Tell as much as you can. Your teacher will listen.

Reading   Look at each picture. Choose a, b, or c. Write the letter on the line.

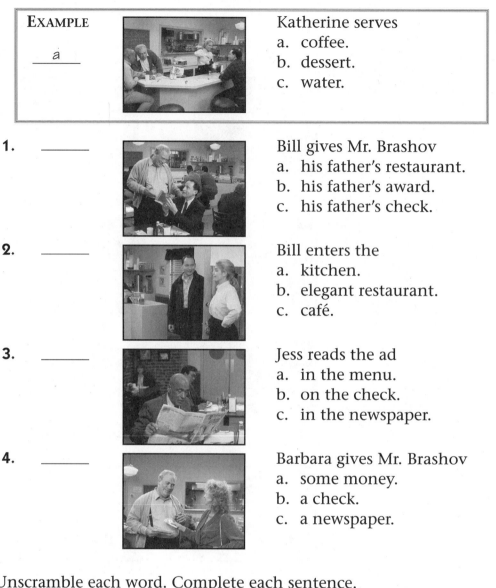

EXAMPLE		Katherine serves
<u>a</u>		a. coffee.
		b. dessert.
		c. water.

1. _____
Bill gives Mr. Brashov
a. his father's restaurant.
b. his father's award.
c. his father's check.

2. _____
Bill enters the
a. kitchen.
b. elegant restaurant.
c. café.

3. _____
Jess reads the ad
a. in the menu.
b. on the check.
c. in the newspaper.

4. _____
Barbara gives Mr. Brashov
a. some money.
b. a check.
c. a newspaper.

Writing   Unscramble each word. Complete each sentence.

EXAMPLE   Katherine serves <u>c</u> <u>o</u> <u>f</u> <u>f</u> <u>e</u> <u>e</u> to Bill.
(o f e e f c)

1. Mr. Brashov has a ___ ___ ___ ___ ___ ___ ___ ___ smile and he
    is friendly. (h r i g n m a c)

2. Barbara wants Mr. Brashov to ___ ___ ___ ___ ___ ___ money.
    (n e s t v i)

3. Jamal has ___ ___ ___ ___ for the camera. (i l f m)

4. Mr. Brashov writes a ___ ___ ___ ___ ___ for $800. (h c k e c)

Name _____   Date _____

Listening   Read each question. Watch the videotape. Circle the letter of the
correct answer.

EXAMPLE	How does Mr. Brashov feel? a. happy b. excited ⓒ worried

1. What are Rosa and Mr. Brashov
   talking about?
   a. dating
   b. working
   c. shopping

2. What is Barbara talking about?
   a. her job
   b. her family
   c. her friends

3. What did Mr. Brashov give Barbara?
   a. some jewelry
   b. some money
   c. some clothing

4. Who is in the photographs Rosa
   shows to Mr. Brashov?
   a. Mr. Brashov and his wife
   b. Barbara and Mr. Brashov
   c. Barbara and another man

5. What does Barbara give back to
   Mr. Brashov?
   a. some pictures
   b. some money
   c. some tickets

Speaking   Talk about this picture. Tell as much as you can. Your teacher will
listen.

Crossroads Café Assessment A

Language Structure   Give compliments.

EXAMPLE	Rosa has a new special.
	This special <u>is delicious.</u>
	OR
	This is <u>a delicious special.</u>

1. Henry has a new jacket.

   Your jacket is _____

2. Katherine has a new dress.

   Your new dress is _____

3. Rosa has new earrings.

   Your new earrings are very _____

4. Your friend has a new haircut.

   Your haircut is _____

5. Your friend has a new car.

   That's a very _____

Critical Thinking   Think about the question below. Write your ideas. Then talk about your ideas. Your teacher will listen.

Do you think telephone salespeople are dishonest? Tell why or why not.

_____

_____

_____

_____

_____

_____

_____

_____

Name _____   Date _____

Listening   Read each question. Watch the videotape. Circle the letter of the correct answer.

EXAMPLE	What does the restaurant need?
	a. more space
	(b.) more customers
	c. more equipment

1. What is Rosa's advice to Mr. Brashov?
   a. He should get some rest.
   b. He should get some exercise.
   c. He should meet some women.

2. What does Barbara say about her job?
   a. She owns a restaurant.
   b. She does advertising.
   c. She works in television.

3. What does Mr. Brashov tell the others?
   a. He gave money to Barbara.
   b. He asked Barbara to marry him.
   c. He sold Crossroads Café.

4. What are Rosa and Jamal saying?
   a. Barbara is not smart.
   b. Barbara is not honest.
   c. Barbara is not good-looking.

5. What is Mr. Brashov trying to do?
   a. get back his money.
   b. lend money to Barbara.
   c. borrow money from Barbara.

Speaking   In this episode, Barbara makes Mr. Brashov believe that she is going to help his business, so he gives her money. This is not true. Barbara just wants Mr. Brashov's money. She is a con artist. Have you or has anyone you know ever met a con artist? Explain what happened. How can you protect yourself from con artists? Tell as much as you can. Your teacher will listen.

Language Structure   Give compliments.

EXAMPLE	Katherine has a new dress.
	<u>Your dress is very pretty.</u>
	OR
	<u>That's a very pretty dress.</u>

1. Mr. Brashov has a new tie.

_____

2. Henry has a new guitar.

_____

3. Rosa has a new apron.

_____

4. Your neighbor has a new sofa.

_____

5. Your friend has a new apartment.

_____

Critical Thinking   Think about the question below. Write your ideas. Then talk about your ideas. Your teacher will listen.

Do you think Mr. Brashov learned a lesson from his experience with Barbara? Tell why or why not.

_____

_____

_____

_____

_____

_____

_____

_____

Name   Date

Listening   Read each question. Watch the videotape. Circle the letter of the correct answer.

EXAMPLE	Why is Mr. Brashov worried? a. There aren't enough employees. b. There aren't enough customers. c. There are problems at home.

1. What does Mr. Brashov say?
   a. He's too old to meet women.
   b. He's too heavy to meet women.
   c. He's too tired to meet women.

2. What is Barbara telling Mr. Brashov?
   a. They can start a new business.
   b. He can help her business.
   c. She can help his business.

3. How do Katherine and Rosa feel?
   a. They are happy about Barbara.
   b. They don't trust Barbara.
   c. They are jealous of Barbara.

4. What do Rosa and Jamal say about Barbara?
   a. She wants Mr. Brashov's money.
   b. She wants to help Mr. Brashov.
   c. She wants to marry Mr. Brashov.

5. What does Mr. Brashov say to Barbara?
   a. They might have a wonderful future together.
   b. They might talk to the police soon.
   c. They might make more deals together.

Speaking   Explain the title, "Let the Buyer Beware," or tell the story. Tell as much as you can. Your teacher will listen.

**Language
Structure**   Give compliments.

EXAMPLE	Rosa made a new dessert.
	This dessert is delicious.
	OR
	This is a delicious dessert.
	OR
	This is a very delicious dessert.

1. Rosa is wearing a new apron.

   _____

2. Jess won a chess game.

   _____

3. Bill likes the name of the café.

   _____

4. A coworker got a promotion.

   _____

5. A friend shows you a picture she painted.

   _____

**Critical
Thinking**   Think about the question below. Write your ideas. Then talk
about your ideas. Your teacher will listen.

*Do you think there are more consumer scams in the United
States than in your native country? Tell why or why not.*

_____

_____

_____

_____

_____

_____

Name _____   Date _____

Reading   Read these ads. Answer the questions.

Ad A

> **Free Special Report!**
>
> Make more than $100,000 a year in Network Marketing. Yes, it's true! You, too, can become one of thousands of people who have discovered financial freedom working in their homes. This special report shows you how. Guaranteed! Call now.
>
> **(800) 645-8887, Ext. 664**

Ad B

> **FREE COMPUTER**
>
> ABC Computer Services needs individuals to run computers part time from their homes. No experience necessary. If you buy our software and training materials, we'll give you a computer, monitor, and printer. If you already have a computer, we'll give you a discount. Call for free video and literature.
>
> **(800) 223-8899, Ext. 1224**

✪ 1. What does ad A promise? _____

2. How much money can you make in Network Marketing? _____

3. What's the phone number to call for ad A? _____

4. What's the name of the company in ad B? _____

5. What do you have to buy in ad B? _____

✪✪ 1. What does the special report in ad A promise? _____

2. What do you have to do to get the report in ad A? _____

3. What is free in ad B? _____

4. How much experience is needed for ad B? _____

5. How much money can you make in ad B? _____

✪✪✪ 1. Write two questions to ask if you called about ad A. _____

_____

2. Write two questions to ask if you called about ad B. _____

_____

3. Which ad sounds too good to be true? Tell why. _____

_____

Writing   In this unit Mr. Brashov was tricked by a woman named Barbara. Write about the things you think Mr. Brashov learned from his experience with Barbara.

Crossroads Café Assessment A   ═══ **10-9**

Learner Checklist

1. Rate yourself.

I CAN . . .	ALWAYS	SOMETIMES	NEVER
give compliments and respond to compliments.	❑	❑	❑
read ads for services.	❑	❑	❑
write a newspaper article.	❑	❑	❑
talk about scams.	❑	❑	❑

2. Meet with your teacher. Talk about how successful you were in reaching the goals for this unit. Compare how you rated yourself with how your teacher rated you.

3. Think about your rating and your teacher's rating. What do you need to study more?

_____

_____

_____

fold -- fold

Instructor Checklist

1. Rate the learner. For each item, circle a number based on the following scale:

3 = easily understood, 2 = understood with difficulty, 1 = not understood

THE LEARNER CAN . . .	RATING	COMMENTS
give compliments and respond to compliments.	1 2 3	
read ads for services.	1 2 3	
write a newspaper article.	1 2 3	
talk about scams.	1 2 3	

2. Meet with the learner. Use the two completed checklists to talk about learner outcomes in this unit and priorities for further study.

Photo Stories

— Listening Answer Key

1. b   **2.** a   **3.** a   **4.** b

— Speaking

Either have students respond to you face to face, or have students record their responses on audiotapes. See Guidelines, page xii, for scoring.

— Reading Answer Key

1. b   **2.** c   **3.** c   **4.** a

— Writing Answer Key

1. charming   **2.** invest   **3.** film   **4.** check

Worktext ✪

— Listening Answer Key

1. a   **2.** a   **3.** b   **4.** c   **5.** b

— Speaking

Either have students respond to you face to face, or have students record their responses on audiotapes. See Guidelines, page xiii, for scoring.

— Language Structure

Answers will vary. See Guidelines, page xvi, for scoring.

1. nice/warm   **2.** nice/pretty   **3.** pretty/nice/stylish   **4.** attractive/modern

5. nice/fast/good/reliable car

— Critical Thinking

Answers will vary. See Guidelines, page x, for scoring.

— Reading Answer Key

Each answer is worth one point.

1. financial freedom

2. more than $100,000 a year

3. 800-645-8887, Ext. 664

4. ABC Computer Services

5. software and training material

— Writing

See Guidelines, page xvii, for scoring.

Worktext ✪✪

— Listening Answer Key

1. c   **2.** b   **3.** a   **4.** b   **5.** a

Speaking

Either have students respond to you face to face, or have students record their responses on audiotapes. If administered face to face and learners are unable to respond, do one of the following:

- move to the one-star assessment for Speaking.
- ask more specific questions about the episode, such as

"What happened when Mr. Brashov met Barbara?" "How did she get him to give her money?"

OR

"How did Barbara take advantage of Mr. Brashov?"

Variation: Ask questions about pictures in Before You Watch (p. 128). For example, point to picture #2 and ask: "What does Mr. Brashov give Barbara?"

See Guidelines, page xiv, for scoring.

Language Structure

Answers will vary; possible answers are provided. See Guidelines, page xvi, for scoring.

1. Your tie is very fashionable/nice. OR That's a nice tie.
2. That's a very nice/good guitar. OR Your guitar is very nice.
3. Your apron is very pretty/colorful. OR That's a very pretty/colorful apron.
4. Your sofa is very nice/comfortable/beautiful. OR That's a very nice/comfortable/beautiful sofa.
5. Your apartment is very large/clean/nice. OR That's a very large/clean/nice apartment.

Critical Thinking

Answers will vary. See Guidelines, page xx, for scoring.

Reading Answer Key

Each answer is worth one point.

1. to show you how to discover financial freedom
2. call
3. video and literature
4. none
5. I don't know. (It doesn't say.)

Writing

Answers will vary. See Guidelines, page xviii, for scoring.

Worktext ✪✪✪

Listening Answer Key

1. a   **2.** c   **3.** b   **4.** a   **5.** b

Speaking

Either have students respond to you face to face, or have students record their responses on audiotapes. If administered face to face and learners are unable to respond, do one of the following:

- move to the two-star assessment for Speaking.
- ask more detailed questions, such as:

  for the meaning of the title

  Who is "the buyer" here?
  Why should Mr. Brashov beware (be careful)?

  for telling the story

  How did Mr. Brashov meet Barbara?
  What did she do to make him trust her?
  How did she use him?
  What did Mr. Brashov's friends do to help?
  How did Mr. Brashov get back his money?

Variation: Have learners respond to general directions such as the following.

  Tell about Barbara's scam.
  Tell about how Mr. Brashov got his money back.
  Explain what con artists do.

See Guidelines, page xv, for scoring.

Language Structure

Answers will vary; possible answers are provided. See Guidelines, page xvi, for scoring.

1. This apron is pretty/colorful. OR This is a (very) pretty/colorful apron.
2. This game is challenging/hard/difficult. OR This is a (very) challenging/hard/difficult game.
3. This name is wonderful/thoughtful. OR This is a wonderful/thoughtful name.
4. This promotion is exciting/good/important. OR The coworker is smart.
5. This painting is beautiful. OR This is a beautiful painting.

Critical Thinking

Answers will vary. See Guidelines, page xx, for scoring.

Reading Answer Key

Answers 1 and 2 are worth two points each; answer 3 is worth one point. Answers may vary.

1. Can you give me the names of people who have bought the report?
   How many people have made over $100,000?
2. Do you guarantee part-time work?
   How much do the software and training materials cost?
3. Both. They make a lot of promises, but they don't give any specific information.

Writing

See Guidelines, page xix, for scoring.

Photo Stories

EXAMPLE	Katherine serves coffee to Bill.

1. Katherine serves dessert to Barbara.
2. Mr. Brashov and Barbara have a date.
3. Katherine and Bill eat at an elegant restaurant.
4. Jamal gives Katherine the film.

Worktext All Levels

EXAMPLE	ROSA:	What's the problem, Mr. Brashov?
	MR. BRASHOV:	This whole week, business has been terrible.
	KATHERINE:	Maybe we should advertise.
	JAMAL:	I could make a big sign for the front of the restaurant. We could have flashing lights, lots of color. I'm sure it would attract a lot of attention.
	KATHERINE:	And probably get us thrown out of the neighborhood.
	ROSA:	Maybe we just need to make the menu a little more exciting. I bought some chili peppers at a vegetable market last weekend. I'm going to put them in tomorrow's chicken special.

1. ROSA: So, what did you do this weekend Mr. Brashov?

   MR. BRASHOV: Well, on Saturday I cleaned up my office. And on Sunday I caught up on some paperwork.

   KATHERINE: Talk about a wild weekend.

   ROSA: Don't you ever have any fun?

   MR. BRASHOV: I run a business here. Who has time for fun?

   ROSA: Mr. Brashov, maybe it's time you started to date.

   MR. BRASHOV: In Romania men of my age do not date.

   ROSA: In Mexico they don't either, but this is America. You just have to get the word out. Let women know you're available.

2. BARBARA: You know, Victor, good food and good service are important to any restaurant, but it's also important to have a good promoter.

MR. BRASHOV: Ah, yes, a promoter. What is a promoter?

BARBARA: It's what I do for a living. I help restaurant owners advertise, so they can get more customers.

MR. BRASHOV: Really?

BARBARA: Yes, I'm good friends with the owner of Palmettos. I helped him win that restaurant award.

MR. BRASHOV: I saw that in the newspaper.

BARBARA: And Victor, I can help you win that award, too.

MR. BRASHOV: But we are not an elegant restaurant like Palmettos. We are just a small neighborhood café . . . with a leaky sprinkler system.

BARBARA: All you need is publicity and advertising.

3. MR. BRASHOV: Barbara says that in this country you can invest one dollar and make one million. But you've got to spend money to make money.

ROSA: What does that mean?

MR. BRASHOV: It means that I invested in Barbara's company. She says Crossroads Café will be known everywhere.

KATHERINE: How can you be so sure that Barbara can do that?

JESS: Don't listen to these two, Victor. They're just giving you a hard time.

MR. BRASHOV: All I know is I am happy and I am going to be successful.

ROSA: I have a bad feeling about that Barbara.

4. MR. BRASHOV: How can this be? I don't understand.

ROSA: Mr. Brashov, this woman is a con artist, a cheat. She uses her charm and good looks to take money from trusting men . . . like you.

MR. BRASHOV: What a fool I've been. I've already given her $800.

JAMAL: These con artists think they can take advantage of anyone who is from another country or speaks with an accent.

HENRY: I bet you'll never see that woman again.

MR. BRASHOV: Oh, yes, I will.

ROSA: How can you be so sure?

MR. BRASHOV: I am supposed to give her another $800. She's coming here tomorrow.

5. MR. BRASHOV: I'll tell you what. For you, Barbara, darling—and please keep this to yourself. You can buy a share of Crossroads Café for only $900.

BARBARA: Make it eight.

MR. BRASHOV: You have a deal.

BARBARA: Oh, Victor, this is so wonderful. I have such great plans for us. The future is full of possibilities.

MR. BRASHOV: The only possibility is that I will call the police if you do not leave in the next minute.

BARBARA: Victor, I don't understand.

MR. BRASHOV: Maybe this will help.

BARBARA: You tricked me, you . . . you. . . .

Name _____   Date _____

Listening   Look at each picture. Listen to the tape. Write the letter of the correct picture on the line.

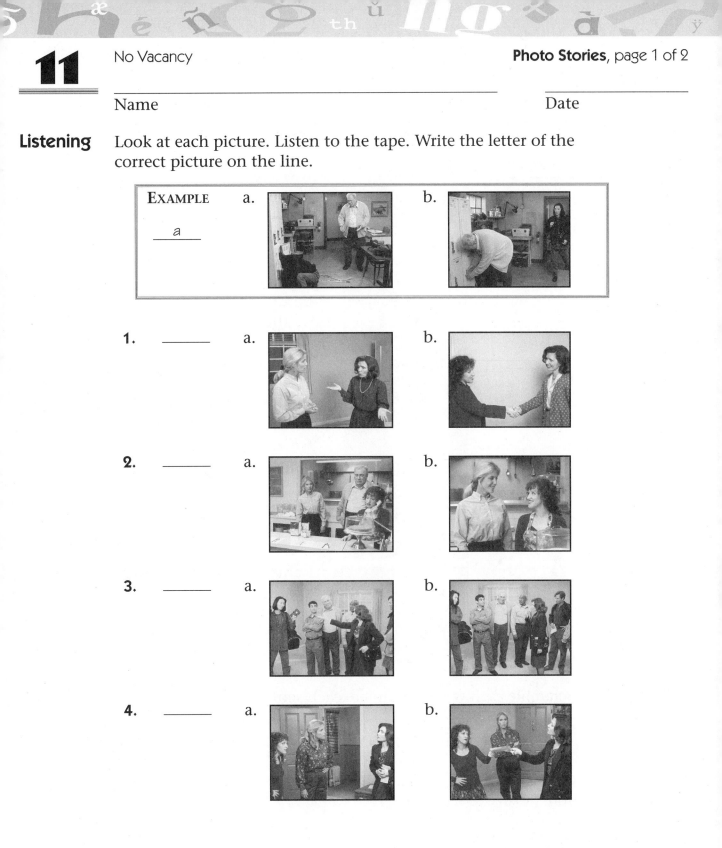

EXAMPLE   a.   b.

_a_

1. _____   a.   b.

2. _____   a.   b.

3. _____   a.   b.

4. _____   a.   b.

Speaking   How do Rosa's friends help? Think about your answer. Tell as much as you can. Your teacher will listen.

Reading   Look at each picture. Choose a, b, or c. Write the letter on the line.

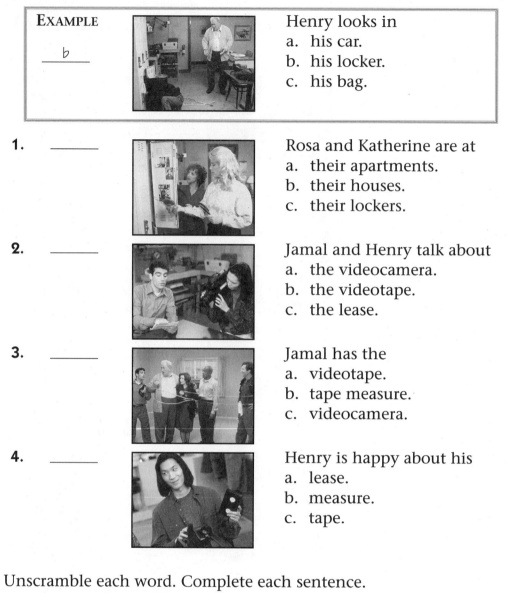

EXAMPLE   _b_

Henry looks in
a. his car.
b. his locker.
c. his bag.

1. _____

Rosa and Katherine are at
a. their apartments.
b. their houses.
c. their lockers.

2. _____

Jamal and Henry talk about
a. the videocamera.
b. the videotape.
c. the lease.

3. _____

Jamal has the
a. videotape.
b. tape measure.
c. videocamera.

4. _____

Henry is happy about his
a. lease.
b. measure.
c. tape.

Writing   Unscramble each word. Complete each sentence.

EXAMPLE   Henry looks in his _l_ _o_ _c_ _k_ _e_ _r_ . (o k r e c l)

1. Rosa uses Katherine as a ___ ___ ___ ___ ___ ___ ___ ___ ___ on the application. (e e e e c n r f r)

2. Dorothy ___ ___ ___ ___ ___ ___ ___ ___ ___ ___ ___ ___ ___ against Rosa because she is from Mexico. (i c i i a e t n m r d s s)

3. Katherine tells Rosa to wait and be ___ ___ ___ ___ ___ ___ ___ . (a i e n t t p)

4. Dorothy wants Patty to sign the ___ ___ ___ ___ ___ for the apartment. (e s e a l)

Name _____   Date _____

Listening Read each question. Watch the videotape. Circle the letter of the correct answer.

EXAMPLE	What is Rosa complaining about?
	(a.) noise
	b. heat
	c. people

1. How does Rosa feel?
   a. worried
   b. confused
   c. excited

2. What is Jess talking about?
   a. discrimination
   b. divorce
   c. drugs

3. Who is Katherine angry at?
   a. Rosa
   b. Mr. Brashov
   c. Ms. Walsh

4. What is Mr. Brashov trying to do?
   a. teach a lesson
   b. tell a joke
   c. play a game

5. How do Katherine and Ms. Walsh feel?
   a. angry and disappointed
   b. happy and excited
   c. sad and depressed

Speaking Talk about this picture. Tell as much as you can. Your teacher will listen.

Language Structure   Ask for clarification.

EXAMPLE	People come in a lot of different packages.
	What do you mean, _different packages?_
	OR
	You mean people are _different?_

1. Henry's video project has to be significant.

    What do you mean, _____

2. There was a little mix-up with Rosa's apartment.

    What do you mean, _____

3. The problem with the apartment manager is not settled.

    What do you mean, _____

4. The apartment manager said, "Rosa's not our type."

    You mean Rosa is _____

5. Your friend is not our type.

    You mean she or he is _____

Critical Thinking   Think about the question below. Write your ideas. Then talk about your ideas. Your teacher will listen.

Do you think Rosa should report the apartment manager to the Fair Housing Bureau? Tell why or why not.

_____

_____

_____

_____

_____

_____

_____

_____

Name _____   Date _____

Listening   Read each question. Watch the videotape. Circle the letter of the correct answer.

EXAMPLE	What is Katherine's advice?
	(a.) Rosa should move.
	b. Rosa should call a plumber.
	c. Rosa should try to fix the pipes herself.

1. What is Rosa doing?
   a. applying to rent an apartment
   b. applying to buy a house
   c. applying for a job

2. Why does Jess think Rosa didn't get the apartment?
   a. because of her job
   b. because of her race
   c. because of her application

3. What is Henry reading?
   a. laws about working
   b. laws about housing
   c. laws about driving

4. Why doesn't Ms. Walsh give the apartment to Mr. Brashov?
   a. because he is a man
   b. because he is very heavy
   c. because he is a foreigner

5. Why is Katherine angry at Ms. Walsh?
   a. She treated the Petersons badly.
   b. She treated Rosa badly.
   c. She treated Katherine badly.

Speaking   In this episode, Rosa did not get an apartment because she was from a different country and she had an accent. This is discrimination, and it is against the law. Did you or anyone else you know experience discrimination when you were looking for an apartment or a job? Why does discrimination happen? Tell as much as you can. Your teacher will listen.

Language Structure Ask for clarification.

EXAMPLE	Discrimination comes in a lot of <u>different packages</u>.
	What do you mean, different packages?
	OR
	You mean discrimination comes in many forms?

1. Henry's video project has to be <u>significant</u>.

   _____

2. You need to push a button to <u>focus</u> the videocamera.

   _____

3. There was <u>a little mix-up</u> with Rosa's apartment.

   _____

4. The apartment manager said, "Rosa's <u>not our type</u>."

   _____

5. Your friend is <u>not wanted here</u>.

   _____

Critical Thinking Think about the question below. Write your ideas. Then talk about your ideas. Your teacher will listen.

Do you think people sometimes judge others by race, color, or gender? Tell why or why not.

   _____

   _____

   _____

   _____

   _____

   _____

   _____

Name _____   Date _____

Listening   Read each question. Watch the videotape. Circle the letter of the correct answer.

EXAMPLE	How does Rosa feel about where she lives?
	(a.) She's getting more and more dissatisfied.
	b. She likes it more now than she did before.
	c. She doesn't mind the few problems she's having.

1. What does Ms. Walsh tell Rosa?
   a. She can have the apartment.
   b. She has to wait a few days.
   c. The apartment is not available.

2. What is Jess saying about discrimination?
   a. Prejudiced people are easy to identify.
   b. Sometimes friendly people are prejudiced.
   c. Discrimination is not really a problem.

3. What is not allowed in the housing code?
   a. discrimination because of people's jobs
   b. discrimination because of people's color
   c. discrimination because of people's income

4. What is Mr. Brashov telling Ms. Walsh?
   a. She is prejudiced.
   b. She is justified.
   c. She is arrested.

5. What does Katherine tell Ms. Walsh?
   a. She is not a friend anymore.
   b. She is not angry anymore.
   c. She is going to move.

Speaking   Explain the title, "No Vacancy," or tell the story. Tell as much as you can. Your teacher will listen.

Language Structure

Ask for clarification.

EXAMPLE	That girl is not quite our type.
	What do you mean, not quite our type?
	OR
	You mean she's not friendly?
	OR
	What does that mean?

1. Rosa's pipes talk to themselves.

2. The apartment manager said that there was a little mix-up.

3. Jess said that discrimination comes in a lot of different packages.

4. Your kind isn't wanted here.

5. Henry's video project had to be socially significant.

Critical Thinking

Think about the question below. Write your ideas. Then talk about your ideas. Your teacher will listen.

Do you think all people have prejudices? Tell why or why not.

Name   Date

Reading   Read the rental application. Answer the questions.

RENTAL APPLICATION	Bank Information

RENTAL APPLICATION
I, _Beth Smith_ , hereby apply to rent Apartment _#304_
at _4040 North Ave_ . Proposed co-resident _Mary Bocconi_
Children: # _0_ Names: _____ N/A _____

APPLICANT INFORMATION
Applicant's name _Beth Smith_ Soc. Sec. # _330-58-1234_
Birth Date _8/14/73_ Valid Dr. Lic. # _____ N/A _____
Address _657 Fifth Ave. Apt. 204_ City/State _Lakeville, IL_
How long? _3 yrs._ Rent per month _$650.00_
Telephone No. _555-6024_ Landlord _Richard Wysocki_
Telephone No. _555-4321_

EMPLOYMENT AND CREDIT INFORMATION
Employment
Employed by _Ace Rent-A-Car_ How long? _1 yr._
Position _reservationist_ Salary _$1400/month_
Address _4532 North Ave._ City/State _Lakeville, IL_
Telephone No. _555-5432_

Bank Information
Bank _Colony Bank_ Branch/City/State _0233 Lakeville, IL_
Checking Account # _14-8521-15_ Savings Account # _77-655_
Major Credit Cards
Name _First Card_ # _7645-1198-4374_
Outstanding Balance _$100.00_
Name _N/A_ # _N/A_
Outstanding Balance _____

REFERENCES
Relative or Friend: _Mark D. Smith_ Relationship _brother_
Address _657 Fifth Ave. Apt. 204_ City/State _Lakeville, IL_
Telephone No. _555-6024_ How long known? _Entire life_
Everything that I have stated in this application is correct to the best of my knowledge. I authorize you to obtain and provide information for the purpose of verification of any part of this rental application.

Date: _Dec. 1, 1996_ Applicant: _Beth Smith_

✪ 1. How long has Beth lived at her current address? _____
2. How much rent does she pay now? _____
3. Where does Beth work? _____
4. How long has she worked at her job? _____
5. What's the name of her bank? _____

✪✪ 1. Whose name does Beth give as a reference? _____
2. What is their relationship? _____
3. How many bank accounts does Beth have? _____
4. How many major credit cards does Beth have? How do you know?
_____

✪✪✪ 1. Does Beth owe any money on her credit cards? How do you know?
_____
2. Can the application information be verified? Tell why or why not.
_____

Writing   In this episode, Rosa tried to rent an apartment, but the apartment manager discriminated against her. You are Rosa. Write a letter to the Fair Housing Bureau to report the discrimination.

Learner Checklist

1. Rate yourself.

I CAN . . .	ALWAYS	SOMETIMES	NEVER
ask for clarification.	❏	❏	❏
read a rental application.	❏	❏	❏
write about discrimination.	❏	❏	❏
talk about causes of discrimination.	❏	❏	❏

2. Meet with your teacher. Talk about how successful you were in reaching the goals for this unit. Compare how you rated yourself with how your teacher rated you.

3. Think about your rating and your teacher's rating. What do you need to study more?

_____

_____

_____

fold _____ fold

Instructor Checklist

1. Rate the learner. For each item, circle a number based on the following scale:

3 = easily understood, 2 = understood with difficulty, 1 = not understood

THE LEARNER CAN . . .	RATING	COMMENTS
ask for clarification.	1 2 3	
read a rental application.	1 2 3	
write about discrimination.	1 2 3	
talk about causes of discrimination.	1 2 3	

2. Meet with the learner. Use the two completed checklists to talk about learner outcomes in this unit and priorities for further study.

Photo Stories

— Listening Answer Key
1. b   **2.** a   **3.** a   **4.** b

— Speaking
Either have students respond to you face to face, or have students record their responses on audiotapes. See Guidelines, page xii, for scoring.

— Reading Answer Key
1. c   **2.** a   **3.** b   **4.** c

— Writing
1. reference   **2.** discriminates   **3.** patient   **4.** lease

Worktext ✪

— Listening Answer Key
1. c   **2.** a   **3.** c   **4.** a   **5.** a

— Speaking
Either have students respond to you face to face, or have students record their responses on audiotapes. See Guidelines, page xiii, for scoring.

— Language Structure
Answers may vary; possible answers are provided. See Guidelines, page xvi, for scoring.
1. significant
2. a little mix-up
3. is not settled
4. Mexican (or other appropriate adjective)
5. (nationality or other appropriate adjective)

— Critical Thinking
Answers will vary. See Guidelines, page xx, for scoring.

— Reading Answer Key
Each answer is worth one point.
1. 3 years   **2.** $ 650   **3.** Ace Rent-A-Car   **4.** 1 year   **5.** Colony Bank

— Writing
Answers will vary. See Guidelines, page xvii, for scoring.

Worktext ✪✪

— Listening Answer Key
1. a   **2.** b   **3.** b   **4.** c   **5.** b

Speaking

Either have students respond to you face to face, or have students record their responses on audiotapes. If administered face to face and learners are unable to respond, do one of the following:

- move to the one-star assessment for Speaking.
- ask more specific questions about the episode, such as:

  "What happened when Rosa applied for an apartment rental?" "Why was she turned down?"

  OR

  "What is discrimination?" "Who gets discriminated against in the episode?"

Variation: Ask questions about pictures in Before You Watch (p. 142). For example, point to picture #1, and ask: "What is Henry doing?"
See Guidelines, page xiv, for scoring.

Language Structure

Answers will vary. See Guidelines, page xvi, for scoring.
1. What do you mean, significant? OR You mean it has to be important/serious?
2. You mean this one?
3. What do you mean, a little mix-up? OR You mean the apartment manager did not like her? OR You mean there was discrimination?
4. You mean Rosa is not American?
5. What do you mean, isn't wanted here? OR You mean he or she is (nationality or other appropriate adjective)?

Critical Thinking

Answers will vary. See Guidelines, page xx, for scoring.

Reading Answer Key

Answers 1, 2, and 3 are worth one point each; answer 4 is worth two points.
1. Mark D. Smith   2. family/brother and sister   3. two   4. one, she wrote N/A on the second line of the major credit card section

Writing

Answers will vary. See Guidelines, page xviii, for scoring.

Worktext ✪✪✪

Listening Answer Key
1. b   2. b   3. b   4. a   5. a

Speaking

Either have students respond to you face to face, or have students record their responses on audiotapes. If administered face to face and learners are unable to respond, do one of the following:

- move to the two-star assessment for Speaking.
- ask more detailed questions, such as:

  <u>for the meaning of the title</u>

  Who was told there was no vacancy?
  Why was Rosa told the apartment was rented?

  <u>for telling the story</u>

  Why did Rosa want to move?
  What happened when she tried to rent an apartment in Katherine's building?
  How did Rosa feel?
  What did Ms. Walsh do that was against the law?
  What did Rosa's friends do to help her?

Variation: Have learners respond to general statements such as the following:

Tell about how Ms. Walsh's treatment of Rosa and the Petersons was different.
Tell about what Henry and the others did to help.
Tell about discrimination laws.

See Guidelines, page xv, for scoring.

Language Structure

Answers will vary. See Guidelines, page xvi, for scoring.
1. You mean they are broken? OR What do you mean, talk to themselves?
2. You mean she did not understand? OR What do you mean, a little mix-up?
3. You mean discrimination comes in many forms? OR What do you mean, different packages?
5. You mean socially important? OR What does socially significant mean?

Critical Thinking

Answers will vary. See Guidelines, page xx, for scoring.

Reading Answer Key

Answer 1 is worth two points; answer 2 is worth three points.
1. Yes, she has an outstanding balance of $100.
2. Yes, because the applicant authorizes the landlord to do it (by signing the rental application).

Writing

Answers will vary. See Guidelines, page xix, for scoring.

Photo Stories

EXAMPLE	Henry looks in his locker.

1. Rosa meets Ms. Walsh the apartment manager.
2. Rosa gets a telephone call about the apartment.
3. Henry shows Ms. Walsh the videotape.
4. Rosa gives Ms. Walsh the lease.

Worktext All Levels

EXAMPLE	ROSA:	The pipes in my apartment. All night long they are making sounds like a science fiction movie.
	KATHERINE:	I don't think I ever saw that movie.
	ROSA:	I can't get any sleep.
	KATHERINE:	Why don't you call your landlord and complain?
	ROSA:	I tried, but all I got was an answering machine so I left a message. My neighbor says they told her they were going to fix it, but she's been saying that for weeks.
	KATHERINE:	Maybe you should move.
	ROSA:	I wouldn't want to desert my roomate . . . but the noises don't seem to bother Carrie at all. You're right . . . maybe I should look for another apartment.

1. **Ms. WALSH:** You've filled out your rental application?

   ROSA: Oh, yes. It's all finished.

   Ms. WALSH: I think you'll be particularly interested in my personal references.

   Ms. WALSH: Oh, I'm sure I will be. Well, everything seems to be in order.

   ROSA: So, when will I know if I get the apartment?

   Ms. WALSH: Rosa, if it were up to me, I'd be helping you unpack right this minute. But unfortunately you are going to have to be patient for a couple of days while we process this application.

   ROSA: Yes, I understand, but I'm so excited. I can stop searching.

2. ROSA: I didn't get it. There was some sort of mix-up. The apartment had already been rented.

JESS: Uh-oh.

MR. BRASHOV: Uh-oh? What is this "uh-oh?"

JESS: I can't tell you how many times in my life I've been told, "I'm sorry, there's been a little mix-up."

ROSA: Oh no, Jess, I know what you are thinking, but it isn't that way at all. Ms. Walsh is very nice. She wanted me to move in. It was just a mistake.

JESS: It could be. But I've been around long enough to know that discrimination comes in a lot of different packages. Now you see it, now you don't.

HENRY: What do you mean, Mr. Washington?

JESS: Prejudice doesn't always come dressed up in a white sheet, Henry, or a black shirt. Most of the time, it wears a handshake and a smile.

3. KATHERINE: . . . and she never even looked at Rosa's application. She'd already made up her mind. "Not quite our type" . . . that's what she said.

JESS: I hate to say I told you so.

MR. BRASHOV: I came to this country to get away from that kind of thinking.

KATHERINE: I couldn't believe that this was the same Ms. Walsh that I've known all this time. You should have heard her call Rosa "the Senorita." It was sickening.

ROSA: I don't want to hear any more. Let's just forget about it.

JAMAL: How can you forget about it, Rosa? That kind of hatred and ignorance is disgusting.

HENRY: It's also illegal. After Rosa got turned down, I contacted the Department of Fair Employment and Housing to check out the laws on discrimination . . . and it's real simple. Section 14040 of the housing code prohibits discrimination based on color, religion, national origin, ancestry, sex or marital status.

4. **Ms. Walsh:** Please!!! The Petersons are getting the apartment. Don't you understand? Your kind is not welcome here.

   Jamal: What do you mean, "our kind?"

   Mr. Brashov: Do you mean because this gentleman is Black? Or do you mean because this gentleman speaks with a funny accent? Like I do.

   Ms. Walsh: Do I have to spell it out?

   Henry: You already have.

   Ms. Walsh: Now what?

   Henry: And it's all here on tape. The Department of Fair Employment and Housing should be very interested in hearing what you just said.

5. **Ms. Walsh:** Oh, so that is what this is all about? Petty revenge? Because Chiquita here didn't get the apartment?

   Katherine: Her name is Rosa. And she's my friend.

   Ms. Walsh: I thought we were friends, Katherine.

   Katherine: Not anymore, Ms. Walsh. I'm going to keep on living here because it wouldn't be fair to my kids to pack them up and move again, but you and I are no longer friends.

   Ms. Walsh: Well, maybe you won't be living here much longer.

   Katherine: Oh, just try and evict me. I'd love to see you in court.

   Rosa: Me, too.

12

Name _____ Date _____

Listening Look at each picture. Listen to the tape. Write the letter of the correct picture on the line.

EXAMPLE a.   b.

_____b_____

1. _____ a.   b.

2. _____ a.   b.

3. _____ a.   b.

4. _____ a.   b.

Speaking What is Edward's problem? Think about your answer. Tell as much as you can. Your teacher will listen.

Reading   Look at each picture. Choose a, b, or c. Write the letter on the line.

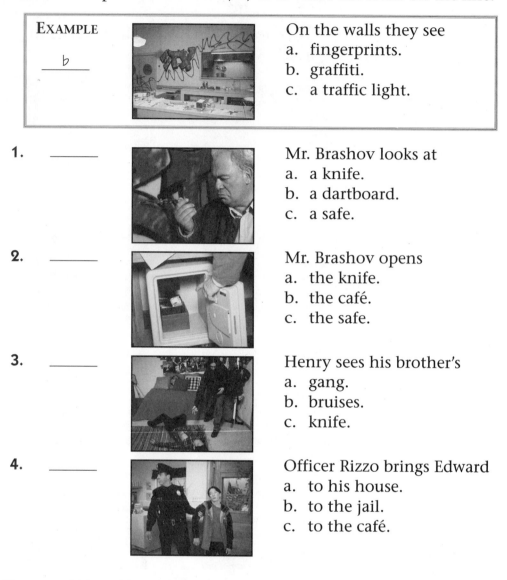

EXAMPLE

__b__

On the walls they see
a. fingerprints.
b. graffiti.
c. a traffic light.

1. _____

Mr. Brashov looks at
a. a knife.
b. a dartboard.
c. a safe.

2. _____

Mr. Brashov opens
a. the knife.
b. the café.
c. the safe.

3. _____

Henry sees his brother's
a. gang.
b. bruises.
c. knife.

4. _____

Officer Rizzo brings Edward
a. to his house.
b. to the jail.
c. to the café.

Writing   Unscramble each word. Complete each sentence.

EXAMPLE   There is __g__ __r__ __a__ __f__ __f__ __i__ __t__ __i__ on the

walls. (r f i i t f a g)

1. After the break-in, Mr. Brashov has to ___ ___ ___ ___ ___ the walls.
   (a n t i p)

2. They didn't take the money, but there was ___ ___ ___ ___ ___ ___.
   (a a e g m d)

3. Edward doesn't join the ___ ___ ___ ___. (g g n a)

4. Mr. Brashov keeps money in a ___ ___ ___ ___. (e a f s)

Name _____   Date _____

Listening Read each question. Watch the videotape. Circle the letter of the correct answer.

EXAMPLE	Who should Rosa give the knife to?
	a. Mr. Brashov
	b. Katherine
	ⓒ Henry

1. What happened to Rosa?
   a. Her car broke down.
   b. Her alarm clock broke.
   c. Her bus was late.

2. How does Henry feel?
   a. angry and worried
   b. surprised and happy
   c. sad and depressed

3. How do Mr. Brashov and Rosa feel when they see the knife?
   a. happy
   b. surprised
   c. angry

4. Who has homework?
   a. Henry
   b. Edward
   c. Edward and Henry

5. What is Edward doing at the café?
   a. visiting Henry
   b. working
   c. playing chess

Speaking Talk about this picture. Tell as much as you can. Your teacher will listen.

Language Structure   Express possibilities.

EXAMPLE	Do you have an umbrella? No. Why?
	It _might rain today._

1. Don't go to the shopping mall alone at night.
   Why not?

   Someone might _____

2. Did you leave the door unlocked?
   Yes.

   Don't go in the house. Someone might be _____

3. I have a headache, a fever, and an upset stomach.

   You might be _____

4. Did you see the graffiti on the sidewalk?

   Yes. It might be _____

5. I hear a dog barking.

   Someone might be _____

Critical Thinking   Think about the question below. Write your ideas. Then talk about your ideas. Your teacher will listen.

Do you think gangs are a problem in your town or city? Tell why or why not.

_____

_____

_____

_____

_____

_____

_____

_____

Crossroads Café Assessment A

_____   _____

Name   Date

Listening   Read each question. Watch the videotape. Circle the letter of the correct answer.

EXAMPLE	What is Rosa going to do with the knife? a. give it to the police (b.) give it to Henry c. give it to Mr. Brashov

1. How does Mr. Brashov feel about Rosa?
   a. He's worried.
   b. He's angry.
   c. He's disappointed.

2. How did Edward get the bruises?
   a. from a beating
   b. from a fall
   c. from a car accident

3. Where did Mr. Brashov see the knife before?
   a. at Henry's house
   b. at the first break-in
   c. at the police station

4. What is Mrs. Chang complaining about?
   a. the noise
   b. the TV
   c. the mess

5. How long will Edward be working at the café?
   a. three weeks
   b. three days
   c. three months

Speaking   In this episode, Henry's brother, Edward, had troubles with a gang. What advice do you have to avoid problems with gangs? Tell as much as you can. Your teacher will listen.

Language Structure Express possibilities.

EXAMPLE	What's the weather going to be like tomorrow?
	It might rain.

1. What are you doing tomorrow?

   _____

2. What are you doing after work?

   _____

3. What classes are you taking next year?

   _____

4. What kind of car do you want to buy?

   _____

5. Where are you going on vacation next summer?

   _____

Critical Thinking Think about the question below. Write your ideas. Then talk about your ideas. Your teacher will listen.

Do you think Edward might have trouble from the gang in the future? Tell why or why not.

_____

_____

_____

_____

_____

_____

_____

_____

_____

Crossroads Café Assessment A

Name   Date

Listening Read each question. Watch the videotape. Circle the letter of the correct answer.

EXAMPLE	Why did the gang put the knife in the wall?
	a. to warn Henry
	(b.) to send a message
	c. to hold a note

1. What promise does Rosa make?
   a. She'll be early tomorrow.
   b. She won't be late again.
   c. She'll stay late.

2. Why didn't Edward tell Henry about the gang?
   a. He didn't want Henry to tell their parents.
   b. He didn't trust Henry.
   c. He didn't think he needed help.

3. Why didn't Henry tell Mr. Brashov about Edward's problems?
   a. He didn't want to bring family problems to work.
   b. He wanted to prove Edward was guilty.
   c. He was afraid of losing his job.

4. Why hasn't Edward told his parents about his problems?
   a. He's afraid they'll be angry.
   b. He doesn't think they can help him.
   c. He doesn't want to hurt them.

5. Why does Henry like having Edward at the café?
   a. Edward is a good worker.
   b. Henry doesn't have to work anymore.
   c. Henry likes to tell him what to do.

Speaking Explain the title, "Turning Points," or tell the story. Tell as much as you can. Your teacher will listen.

Language Structure   Express possibilities.

EXAMPLE	What are your specials today, Rosa?
	I might cook Monterey Chicken.

1. What are you eating for dinner tonight?

   _____

2. What are your plans for the weekend?

   _____

3. Why are you reading the used car ads?

   _____

4. What time are the neighbors coming to the party?

   _____

5. Why are the Changs meeting with a real estate agent?

   _____

Critical Thinking   Think about the question below. Write your ideas. Then talk about your ideas. Your teacher will listen.

Edward had to work for three weeks at the café to pay for the damages. Do you think that was fair? Tell why or why not.

_____

_____

_____

_____

_____

_____

_____

_____

_____

_____

Name _____   Date _____

Reading

Read the police report from the newspaper. Circle Yes or No.

Sunset Hills

• A resident in the 200 block of Coe Street told police vandals damaged a fence outside the residence late Saturday. Damage was estimated at $300.

• Residents in the 100 block of Mohawk Lane told police that someone drove a vehicle over at least one lawn on Sunday night. Damage was estimated at $200.

• Police said they arrested a 53-year-old man Monday after he stabbed a 31-year-old woman in the arm. The victim was taken to Glen Oaks Hospital. The man was charged with aggravated battery.

Oak Forest

• A 21-year-old man was arrested at Nordeen's Department Store on Sunday. He was accused of leaving the store without paying for a $345 jacket. Police charged the man with retail theft.

• A 35-year-old man was arrested last week after an attack on a 27-year-old woman. The assailant was charged with battery and released on bond.

✪ 1. Someone stole a jacket.   YES   NO
   2. Someone stole a fence.   YES   NO
   3. Someone stabbed a woman in the face.   YES   NO
   4. One person was arrested.   YES   NO
   5. One lawn was damaged.   YES   NO

✪✪ 1. Teenagers committed all of the crimes.   YES   NO
   2. Only one person was injured.   YES   NO
   3. The damage to the fence was $300.   YES   NO
   4. A house was robbed.   YES   NO
   5. The youngest victim was 27 years old.   YES   NO

✪✪✪ 1. All of the crimes were on the weekend.   YES   NO
   2. Only one criminal was released on bond. YES   NO
   3. Both of the battery victims were women. YES   NO
   4. The police arrested criminals for all of the crimes. YES NO
   5. The criminals were all under 50-years old. YES NO

Writing

In this unit, Henry and his friends at Crossroads Café worked together to fight the neighborhood gang. Does your neighborhood have gang problems? Write about why or why not.

Learner Checklist

1. Rate yourself.

I can . . .	ALWAYS	SOMETIMES	NEVER
express possibilities.	❏	❏	❏
read a police crime log.	❏	❏	❏
write a newspaper article.	❏	❏	❏
talk about solutions to gang problems.	❏	❏	❏

2. Meet with your teacher. Talk about how successful you were in reaching the goals for this unit. Compare how you rated yourself with how your teacher rated you.

3. Think about your rating and your teacher's rating. What do you need to study more?

_____

_____

_____

fold --- fold

Instructor Checklist

1. Rate the learner. For each item, circle a number based on the following scale:

3 = easily understood, 2 = understood with difficulty, 1 = not understood

THE LEARNER CAN . . .	RATING	COMMENTS
express possibilities.	1 2 3	
read a police crime log.	1 2 3	
write a newspaper article.	1 2 3	
talk about solutions to gang problems.	1 2 3	

2. Meet with the learner. Use the two completed checklists to talk about learner outcomes in this unit and priorities for further study.

Photo Stories

— Listening Answer Key
1. a   **2.** b   **3.** a   **4.** b

— Speaking
Either have students respond to you face to face, or have students record their responses on audiotapes. See Guidelines, page xii, for scoring.

— Reading Answer Key
1. a   **2.** c   **3.** b   **4.** c

— Writing Answer Key
1. paint   **2.** damage   **3.** gang   **4.** safe

Worktext ✪

— Listening Answer Key
1. c   **2.** a   **3.** b   **4.** b   **5.** b

— Speaking
Either have students respond to you face to face, or have students record their responses on audiotapes. See Guidelines, page xiii, for scoring.

— Language Structure
Answers may vary; possible answers are provided. See Guidelines, page xvi, for scoring.
1. attack you
2. inside
3. sick
4. neighbors
5. at the door; outside

— Critical Thinking
Answers will vary. See Guidelines, page xx, for scoring.

— Reading Answer Key
Each answer is worth one point.
1. Yes   **2.** No   **3.** No   **4.** No   **5.** Yes

— Writing
Answers will vary. See Guidelines, page xvii, for scoring.

Worktext ✪✪

— Listening Answer Key
1. a   **2.** a   **3.** b   **4.** a   **5.** a

— Speaking

Either have students respond to you face to face, or have students record their responses on audiotapes. If administered face to face and learners are unable to respond, do one of the following:

- move to the one-star assessment for Speaking.
- ask more specific questions about the episode, such as

  "What did Mr. Brashov find when he opened the café one morning?"
  "How did Henry find out his bother was involved with the break-in?"
  "How did Edward help the police catch the gang?"

Variation: Ask questions about pictures in Before You Watch (p. 156). For example, point to picture #1 and ask, "Who is in the café?"
See Guidelines, page xiv, for scoring.

— Language Structure

Answers may vary; possible answers are provided. See Guidelines, page xvi, for scoring.

1. I'm going shopping.
2. I am going out with some friends.
3. I am taking computer science and biology.
4. I want to buy a new Honda.
5. I am going to New Mexico.

— Critical Thinking

Answers will vary. See Guidelines, page xx, for scoring.

— Reading Answer Key

1. No   **2.** No   **3.** Yes   **4.** No   **5.** Yes

— Writing

Answers will vary. See Guidelines, page xviii, for scoring.

Worktext ✪✪✪

— Listening Answer Key

1. b   **2.** c   **3.** a   **4.** b   **5.** c

— Speaking

Either have students respond to you face to face, or have students record their responses on audiotapes. If administered face to face and learners are unable to respond, do one of the following:

- move to the two-star assessment for Speaking.

- ask more detailed questions, such as the following:

  <u>for the meaning of the title</u>

  What is a turning point?
  What was the turning point for Edward?
  What was the turning point for Mr. Brashov?

  <u>for telling the story</u>

  What did Mr. Brashov see when he opened the café?
  What did he do?
  What did he find on the wall? Why was this important?
  What problems did Edward have?
  What did Mr. Brashov do to stop the gang?

Variation: Have learners respond to general directions such as:

Tell me about Edward's relationship with his parents.
Tell me how Edward helped the police.
Tell me how Mr. Brashov's neighbors helped him.

See Guidelines, page xv, for scoring.

Language Structure

Answers may vary; possible answers are provided. See Guidelines, page xvi, for scoring.

1. We might have spaghetti.
2. I might go to Chicago.
3. I might buy a car.
4. They might come late.
5. They might buy a house. OR They might sell a house.

Critical Thinking

Answers will vary. See Guidelines, page xx, for scoring.

Reading Answer Key

Each answer is worth one point.

1. No   2. Yes   3. Yes   4. No   5. No

Writing

Answers will vary. See Guidelines, page xix, for scoring.

Photo Stories

EXAMPLE	There is graffiti on the walls.

1. Mr. Brashov talks to a police officer.
2. Jamal teaches Rosa to drive.
3. The gang comes to the café.
4. The police take the gang to jail.

Worktext All Levels

EXAMPLE	MR. BRASHOV:	Look at this. It has Chinese lettering on it.
	ROSA:	Henry must have left it here when he was opening boxes.
	MR. BRASHOV:	What is it doing in the wall?
	ROSA:	I don't know. Maybe they wanted to show us they could do whatever they want to our property. What shall we do with it?
	MR. BRASHOV:	Oh, just give it back to Henry.

1. MR. BRASHOV: Katherine, do you know why Rosa isn't here yet?

   KATHERINE: Well, it's got to be one of four things. Either her roommate's car is in the shop, they turned off the water in her building, her alarm clock died, or . . .

   ROSA: I'm sorry. My bus was late.

   KATHERINE: That was my next guess.

   ROSA: But it won't happen again.

   KATHERINE: You're right. It won't.

   MR. BRASHOV: It won't?

   KATHERINE: No.

2. EDWARD: Wait! Everyday they've been messing with me.

   HENRY: Who?

   EDWARD: These guys. They say if I don't do what they tell me, they're going to keep beating me up even worse.

   HENRY: What are you talking about?

EDWARD: A couple of weeks ago they wanted money. Then they wanted me to take something from the principal's office. And then it was breaking into the restaurant.

HENRY: Why?

EDWARD: They said it was part of joining.

HENRY: What are you doing hanging around with a gang?

EDWARD: I didn't want to. They said if I didn't join, they were going to keep beating me up.

HENRY: Why didn't you tell me.

EDWARD: I wanted to take care of it myself.

3. POLICE: Is this your brother?

HENRY: Yes.

MR. BRASHOV: Officer Rizzo, there must be some mistake.

POLICE: No, I don't think so. We found this on him when we picked him up. Have you seen this knife before?

MR. BRASHOV: Yes. It's the same one we found in the back after the break-in.

HENRY: I didn't want to bring my family's problems in to the restaurant.

MR. BRASHOV: Henry, we are not like strangers here.

HENRY: I know. But it's not the same thing.

4. MRS. CHANG: What is going on in here?

EDWARD: Nothing.

MRS. CHANG: Well could you do nothing a little more quietly?

HENRY: Sorry.

MRS. CHANG: Edward, have you finished your homework yet?

EDWARD: Almost.

MRS. CHANG: Your father wants to check it over when you're through. Henry, could you teach your brother something useful?

HENRY: Maybe you should tell them what happened.

EDWARD: It wouldn't do any good. Any time there's a problem with outsiders, all they do is smile and look down.

HENRY: Wrong. You have no idea what you're talking about. They've had to stand up to much more than anyone in that stupid gang ever will. All right. Come on. Your turn.

5. **EDWARD:** Okay. I've washed all the pots and pans. Now what?

HENRY: Clean up the stove, then the refrigerator. And when you're finished with that, start mopping the floor.

KATHERINE: How long does your brother have to work here?

HENRY: Mr. Brashov said three weeks would be enough to pay for all of the damages.

KATHERINE: That seems fair.

HENRY: Well, I was hoping it would be a little longer than that.

KATHERINE: Why?

HENRY: I'm really going to miss bossing him around.

Name _____ Date _____

Listening Look at each picture. Listen to the tape. Write the letter of the correct picture on the line.

EXAMPLE	a.	b.
_a_		

1. _____ a. b.

2. _____ a. b.

3. _____ a. b.

4. _____ a. b.

Speaking Who trades places? Think about your answer. Tell as much as you can. Your teacher will listen.

Reading   Look at each picture. Choose a, b, or c. Write the letter on the line.

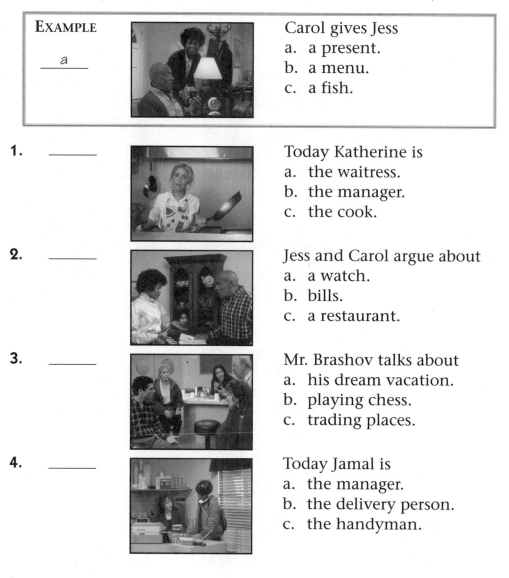

EXAMPLE		Carol gives Jess
_a_		a. a present.
		b. a menu.
		c. a fish.

1. _____   Today Katherine is
a. the waitress.
b. the manager.
c. the cook.

2. _____   Jess and Carol argue about
a. a watch.
b. bills.
c. a restaurant.

3. _____   Mr. Brashov talks about
a. his dream vacation.
b. playing chess.
c. trading places.

4. _____   Today Jamal is
a. the manager.
b. the delivery person.
c. the handyman.

Writing   Unscramble each word. Complete each sentence.

EXAMPLE	Carol gave Jess a _p_ _r_ _e_ _s_ _e_ _n_ _t_ .
	(n e t s e p r)

1. Mr. Brashov wants to catch a big ___ ___ ___ ___ on his vacation.
(s i f h)

2. Switch and change are other words for ___ ___ ___ ___ ___.
(t e r a d)

3. Jess says they can't ___ ___ ___ ___ ___ ___ to eat out because he isn't working. (f r a d o f)

4. Jess and Carol ___ ___ ___ ___ ___ about their bills. (a e g r u)

Name   Date

Listening   Read each question. Watch the videotape. Circle the letter of the
correct answer.

EXAMPLE   What are Jess and Mr. Brashov talking about?
    ⓐ. a vacation
    b. a dream
    c. some advice

1. What are Katherine and Rosa doing?
   a. working
   b. agreeing
   c. arguing

2. What are Jess and Carol talking
   about?
   a. work
   b. shopping
   c. food

3. What is Mr. Brashov talking about?
   a. The job Jamal will do.
   b. The job Henry will do.
   c. The job Katherine will do.

4. How does Henry feel about
   Katherine's special?
   a. disappointed
   b. pleased
   c. surprised

5. What are Jess and Mr. Brashov talking
   about?
   a. his experiment
   b. the lunch crowd
   c. tough jobs

Speaking   Talk about this picture. Tell as much as you can. Your teacher will
listen.

Language Structure Answer the questions.

EXAMPLE	What can Rosa do?
	cook

1. What can Jamal do?

   _____

2. Can Jess and Carol afford to eat out?

   _____

3. What languages can Katherine speak?

   _____

4. What languages can you speak?

   _____

5. What else can you do?

   _____

Critical Thinking Think about the question below. Write your ideas. Then talk about your ideas. Your teacher will listen.

Do you think trading places is easy? Tell why or why not.

   _____

   _____

   _____

   _____

   _____

   _____

   _____

   _____

   _____

   _____

Name _____   Date _____

Listening   Read each question. Watch the videotape. Circle the letter of the correct answer.

EXAMPLE	What is Jess's advice to Mr. Brashov?
	(a.) to take a vacation
	b. to wait to take a vacation
	c. not to take a vacation

1. Who is most important?
   a. the cook
   b. the waitress
   c. everyone

2. Where has Carol been?
   a. working late
   b. shopping for food
   c. buying a gift

3. What is Jamal worried about?
   a. taking over for Henry
   b. who will fix things
   c. Mr. Brashov's skills as a handyman

4. What can you tell about Katherine's special?
   a. Henry thinks it is special.
   b. A customer ordered it.
   c. Katherine wants to keep it simple.

5. Why is the lunch crowd important?
   a. A lot of customers will make employees' jobs more difficult.
   b. A lot of customers will make more money for Mr. Brashov.
   c. A lot of customers will help Mr. Brashov's experiment.

Speaking   This episode was about trading places. Jess and Carol traded places and the workers traded places. Have you ever traded places? Has anyone you know ever traded places? Choose one question. Think about what happened. Tell as much as you can. Your teacher will listen.

Language Structure Answer the questions.

EXAMPLE	What can Jamal do?
	He can fix things.

1. Can you speak Russian?

   _____

2. What languages can you speak?

   _____

3. What do Jess and Mr. Brashov know how to do?

   _____

4. Does Carol know how to add and subtract?

   _____

5. What do you know how to do?

   _____

Critical Thinking Think about the questions below. Write your ideas. Then talk about your ideas. Your teacher will listen.

Why do you think Mr. Brashov had a heart attack? What would you tell him to do differently so he doesn't have another one?

_____

_____

_____

_____

_____

_____

_____

_____   _____
Name   Date

Listening   Read each question. Watch the videotape. Circle the letter of the correct answer.

> EXAMPLE   What does Mr. Brashov think about taking a vacation?
> a. He can take one now because there is not much work to do.
> b. It's just a dream because there's always something to fix.
> c. He will take one when the time is right.

1. What does Mr. Brashov tell Katherine and Rosa to do?
   a. to decide who is important
   b. to stop arguing
   c. to trade jobs

2. How does Jamal feel?
   a. He's disappointed.
   b. He's pleased.
   c. He's surprised.

3. What does Katherine think of Mr. Brashov as a handyman?
   a. She thinks he isn't very good.
   b. She thinks he is as good as Jamal.
   c. She thinks he is better than Jamal.

4. Why did Katherine choose a turkey sandwich as her special?
   a. because a customer ordered it
   b. because Henry thinks it is special
   c. because she thinks it is simple to make

5. What does Mr. Brashov think is going to happen?
   a. Nothing will change.
   b. Things will get more difficult.
   c. Things will get easier.

Speaking   Explain the title, "Trading Places," or tell the story. Tell as much as you can. Your teacher will listen.

Crossroads Café Assessment A   ═══ **13-7**

Language Structure Answer the questions.

EXAMPLE	Does Rosa know how to speak Spanish?
	Yes, she does.

1. Can you play chess?

   _____

2. What other games can you play?

   _____

3. Do you know how to cook?

   _____

4. What else do you know how to do?

   _____

5. Write a question using *can* or *know how to.*

   _____

Critical Thinking Think about the question below. Write your ideas. Then talk about your ideas. Your teacher will listen.

Are the roles of people in your family the same in this country as they were in your native country? Tell how they are the same or different.

_____

_____

_____

_____

_____

_____

_____

_____

Name   Date

Reading   Read the Help Wanted ads. Check (✓) Yes or No.

✪ **Chef—cafeteria F/T**
Producing sandwiches, salads, and cold/hot food. Exp. nec. Able to manage people.
Call Ed 217/555-0602

	Yes	No
EXAMPLE A caféteria serves food.	✓	
1. This chef makes hot food only.		
2. You need to call Ed to apply for the job.		
3. The job is part time.		
4. Experience is necessary.		
5. You need to be good with people.		

✪✪ Receptionist P/T for hair salon. Heavy phone, cashiering & light bookkeeping. Exp. pref'd. Benefits. Apply in person mornings at 4835 Main. No phone calls.

	Yes	No
1. Experience is required.		
2. The job is part-time.		
3. This job has no benefits.		
4. This receptionist will do a lot of bookkeeping.		
5. Apply for this job before noon only.		

✪✪✪ RETAIL SALES POSITION Computer Store. Full time. Knowledgeable. Gd with customers. Gd communication skills. Exc. pay. Full health & dental.
Fax résumé 217/555-6498.

	Yes	No
1. This job provides benefits.		
2. You apply by telephone.		
3. You need to be good with people.		
4. The pay is not very good.		
5. You need to know computers.		

Writing   In this unit, Jess wrote a note of apology to Carol. Now you write a note of apology for this situation: *A friend invited you to a party last Saturday night. You accepted, but you did not go.*

Learner Checklist

1. Rate yourself.

I CAN . . .	ALWAYS	SOMETIMES	NEVER
talk about my abilities.	❏	❏	❏
get information from help wanted ads.	❏	❏	❏
write a note of apology.	❏	❏	❏
talk about roles of husbands and wives.	❏	❏	❏

2. Meet with your teacher. Talk about how successful you were in reaching the goals for this unit. Compare how you rated yourself with how your teacher rated you.

3. Think about your rating and your teacher's rating. What do you need to study more?

_____

_____

_____

fold --- fold

Instructor Checklist

1. Rate the learner. For each item, circle a number based on the following scale:

3 = easily understood, 2 = understood with difficulty, 1 = not understood

THE LEARNER CAN . . .	RATING	COMMENTS
talk about abilities.	1 2 3	
get information from help wanted ads.	1 2 3	
write a note of apology.	1 2 3	
talk about roles of husbands and wives.	1 2 3	

2. Meet with the learner. Use the two completed checklists to talk about learner outcomes in this unit and priorities for further study.

Photo Stories

— Listening Answer Key
1. b   **2.** a   **3.** a   **4.** a

— Speaking
Either have students respond to you face to face, or have students record their responses on audiotapes. See Guidelines, page xii, for scoring.

— Reading Answer Key
1. c   **2.** b   **3.** c   **4.** b

— Writing Answer Key
1. fish   **2.** trade   **3.** afford   **4.** argue

Worktext ✪

— Listening Answer Key
1. a   **2.** b   **3.** b   **4.** c   **5.** a

— Speaking
Either have students respond to you face to face, or have them record their responses on audiotapes. See Guidelines, page xiii, for scoring.

— Language Structure
Answers may vary; possible answers are provided. See Guidelines, page xvi, for scoring.
1. fix things
2. No, they can't. OR Yes, they can.
3. English
4. student's language
5. speak English

— Critical Thinking
Answers will vary. See Guidelines, page xx, for scoring.

— Reading Answer Key
Each answer is worth 1 point.
1. no   **2.** yes   **3.** no   **4.** yes   **5.** yes

— Writing
Answers will vary. See Guidelines, page xvii, for scoring.

Worktext ✪✪

— Listening Answer Key
1. b   **2.** c   **3.** a   **4.** c   **5.** b

Speaking

Either have students respond to you face to face, or have them record their responses on audiotapes. If administered face to face and learners are unable to respond, do one of the following:

- move to the one-star assessment for Speaking.
- ask more specific questions about the episode, such as:

  "Tell me what happened when Jess and Carol traded places."
  OR
  "Tell me what happened when the workers traded places."

Variation: Ask questions about pictures in Before You Watch (page 170). For example, point to picture #1 and ask, *"Who is in this picture? What does he usually do at Crossroads Café? What does he do in this episode?"*
See Guidelines, page xiv, for scoring.

Language Structure

Answers may vary; possible answers are provided. See Guidelines, page xvi, for scoring.

1. Yes, I can. OR No, I can't.
2. I can speak (student's own language).
3. They know how to play chess.
4. Yes, she does.
5. I know how to speak English.

Critical Thinking

Answers will vary. See Guidelines, page xx, for scoring.

Reading Answer Key

Each answer is worth one point.

1. no   2. yes   3. no   4. no   5. yes

1.5 points (1.0 for content and 0.5 for mechanics) for each question written for the "Don't Know" columns checked:
Possible questions for item 2:
   What are the benefits? What benefits are included? Please tell me about the benefits.
Possible questions for item 3:
   What is the pay? Please tell me about the pay. How much is the pay?

Writing

Answers will vary. See Guidelines, page xviii, for scoring.

Worktext ✪✪✪

Listening Answer Key

1. c   2. c   3. a   4. c   5. b

Speaking

Either have students respond to you face to face, or have them record their responses on audiotapes. If administered face to face and learners are unable to respond, do one of the following:

- move to the two-star assessment for Speaking.
- ask more detailed questions, such as:

  for the meaning of the title

  Who traded places at the café?
  Was it easy for them to trade places?
  How have Carol and Jess traded places?
  How does Jess feel about their changed roles?

  for telling the story

  Why doesn't Mr. Brashov take a vacation?
  What is Mr. Brashov's idea?
  Why does he think it is a good idea?
  How do the workers do when they change jobs?
  How do Jess and Carol get along?
  What do they fight about?
  Why do they fight?
  What do the workers and Jess and Carol learn about trading places?

Variation: Have learners respond to general directions such as the following.

Tell me about Mr. Brashov's idea.
Tell me about Jess and Carol.
Tell me what happens when the employees change places.
Tell me why Carol visited Jess at the café.

See Guidelines, page xv, for scoring.

Language Structure

Answers may vary; possible answers are provided. See Guidelines, page xvi, for scoring.

1. Yes, I can. OR No, I can't.
2. I can play (name of game).
3. Yes, I do. OR No, I don't.
4. I know how to (verb).
5. Can you __speak Chinese__? OR Do you know how to __speak Chinese__?

Critical Thinking

Answers will vary. See Guidelines, page xx, for scoring.

Reading Answer Key

Each answer is worth one point.

1. yes   2. no   3. yes   4. no   5. yes

Writing

Answers will vary. See Guidelines, page xix, for scoring.

Photo Stories

EXAMPLE	Carol and Jess argue.

1. Henry drops a customer's food.
2. Rosa gives a customer change.
3. Carol gives Jess a gift.
4. Mr. Brashov talks about his dream vacation.

Worktext All Levels

EXAMPLE	MR. BRASHOV:	You see, there is so much work to do in the café. How can I take a vacation?
	JESS:	You want my advice?
	MR. BRASHOV:	Do I have a choice?
	JESS:	There's always something to fix. Go on this vacation now, or it will always be just a dream.
	MR. BRASHOV:	When the time is right, I will go.

1. MR. BRASHOV: This restaurant would not be open if you did not do those other jobs.

    ROSA: Like my cooking, for example. How can you have a restaurant without a cook?

    KATHERINE: How can you have a restaurant without a waitress?

    MR. BRASHOV: Katherine, Rosa. Stop. Everyone is important here. Everyone is equal at Crossroads Café.

2. CAROL: Hi, Jess.

    JESS: Where have you been? Working late again?

    CAROL: Actually, I went shopping.

    JESS: I thought you did that yesterday.

    CAROL: Yesterday was for food. Today was for something else.

    JESS: What's this?

    CAROL: It's the something else I went shopping for.

3. **MR. BRASHOV:** And Jamal, you will take over from Henry. You will bus the tables and also make the deliveries.

JAMAL: Mr. Brashov, who will take my place? Who will fix things around here?

MR. BRASHOV: I know how to fix things. I will be the handyman.

KATHERINE: Let's hope nothing breaks.

4. **KATHERINE:** There you go, Henry, one "Katherine's Special."

HENRY: But the customer ordered a turkey sandwich!

KATHERINE: Yes, and today, that's my special.

HENRY: A turkey sandwich doesn't sound very special to me.

KATHERINE: Hey, it's my first day as cook. I'm trying to keep things simple. OK?

5. **JESS:** Well, Victor, it looks like your experiment is really working out.

MR. BRASHOV: We will know soon, my friend.

JESS: What do you mean?

MR. BRASHOV: In fifteen seconds, the lunch crowd will be here, and then my employees will see just how tough these jobs really are.

JESS: Maybe they won't all come.

MR. BRASHOV: Oh, they will. They always do.